OVERTHINKING

The Simple 3-Step System to Shut Up Your Thoughts and Rewire Your Brain for Success. Declutter Your Mind and Instantly Overcome Anxiety with Self-Discipline and Mindfulness Techniques

2 BOOKS IN 1

>> *Special Bonus on the last page!*

Table of Contents

BOOK 1: MENTAL TOUGHNESS AND SELF-DISCIPLINE

CHAPTER 1: UNDERSTANDING MENTAL TOUGHNESS 9
- The Four Dimensions of Mental Toughness... 10
  - Hope 13
  - Confidence... 14
  - Perseverance 15
  - Resilience... 16
- The Link Between Mental Toughness & Success.................................. 17
- Are You Mentally Tough? 19

CHAPTER 2: THE SPARTAN WAY 21
- The Dog You Feed 22
- The Fear of Uncertainty... 26
- Comfort in Victimhood... 28
- Nothing Happens Until You Move... 30

CHAPTER 3: THE PSYCHOLOGY OF WILLPOWER, MOTIVATION, AND DISCIPLINE.. 32
- Self- Awareness.. 35
- The David Vs Goliath Complex 38
- Ditching Bad Habits... 40

CHAPTER 4: GRIT AND RESILIENCE 43
- The No-Surrender Mindset 44
- Disrupting Yourself 47
- Stop Making Emotional Decisions 50

CHAPTER 5: TURNAROUND TOUGHNESS 52
- Acceptance 53
- Processing the Truth 56
- Learning from Failure 58
- Moving On 61

CHAPTER 6: CRITICAL MOMENT TOUGHNESS 65
Calmness Under Fire 67
The Power of Positive Thinking 73
Staying in Your Lane 79
It Starts with Self-Belief 83

CHAPTER 7: ENDURANCE TOUGHNESS 86
Perseverance; The Science of Not Giving Up 88
Be Where Your Feet Are 94
Trust Your Journey 98

CHAPTER 8. RISK MANAGEMENT TOUGHNESS 103
Overcoming the Fear of Failure 105
The Perfection Fallacy 113
Beating Procrastination 118

CHAPTER 9: NAVY SEAL STRATEGIES FOR MENTAL TOUGHNESS AND SELF-DISCIPLINE 123
Push Yourself 125
Adapt and Keep It Moving 127
Visualize your Success 131
Self-Affirmation 132
Keep Your Eyes on the Ball 134

CHAPTER 10: WHAT DOES MENTAL STRENGTH LOOK LIKE 137
Ten Things That Mentally Strong People Do Not Do 137
The Systemic Approach to Mental Strength 146

CONCLUSION 151

BOOK 2: PROCRASTINATION 153
INTRODUCTION 154
CHAPTER 1: THE ART OF PLAYING CATCH UP 156

TYPES OF PROCRASTINATION	158
THE STAGES OF PROCRASTINATION	163
WHAT IS PROCRASTINATION COSTING YOU	166
ARE YOU A PROCRASTINATOR?	169

CHAPTER 2: WHY DO YOU PROCRASTINATE 171

THE PERFECTIONIST	172
THE DREAMER	175
THE OCTOPUS	176
THE PLEASURE SEEKER	178
THE GOLDFISH	180

CHAPTER 3: THE OVERTHINKING TRAP 183

MAKING MOUNTAINS OUT OF MOLEHILLS	184
NEGATIVE SELF-TALK	187
GET OUT OF YOUR HEAD	192
DEVELOPING A BIAS TOWARDS ACTION	197

CHAPTER 4: HOW LAZY ARE YOU? 200

THE PLEASURE PRINCIPLE	201
INVESTING IN THE PROCESS	210
MASTERING SELF-REGULATION	214

CHAPTER 5: GET A GRIP 218

THE EMOTIONAL NATURE OF PROCRASTINATION	218
THE CURSE OF INACTION	221
WHY TOMORROW IS TOO LATE	223
OVERCOMING YOUR FEAR	224

CHAPTER 6: THE OCTOPUS MYTH 228

THE CURSE OF URGENT	230
MANAGING STRESS AND BURNOUT	234
OPTIMIZE YOUR ENVIRONMENT FOR PRODUCTIVITY	241

CHAPTER 7: MENTAL MODELS 245

- Are you Limited by Your Thoughts? 246
- Re-Framing Your Mental Models 250
- The Decision-Making Process 257

CHAPTER 8: STAYING FOCUSED 262
- Negative Energy 264
- Ditching Bad Habits 268
- Getting Comfortable with Uncertainty 273
- Advice from Your Future Self 277

CHAPTER 9: HABITS FOR SUCCESS 281
- Stop Self-Sabotage 282
- Declutter Your Mind 286
- Instant Gratification Isn't So Gratifying 289
- Develop Self-Discipline 290

CHAPTER 10: A NEW BEGINNING; YOUR TOOLS AT A GLANCE 293
- The Power of Self Awareness 294
- Maintaining Focus and Motivation 296
- Time Management Strategies 298
- Psychological Tricks to Stop Procrastinating 299

CONCLUSION 302

BOOK 1:
Mental Toughness & Self-Discipline

The Simple 4-Step Framework of NAVY SEALS and SPARTAN WARRIORS to Unfu*k Your Mind and Rewire Your Brain for SUCCESS.

Ready to Unleash Your Maximum Potential?

Introduction

The allure of the low hanging fruits is not that they are the ripest fruits on the tree but rather that they are the easiest to reach. This in a nutshell defines the way most people live their lives. Always seeking the shortest route, the easiest solution, and the quickest results.

We have been programmed by society, by life, and by our emotions to seek comfort and security above all else. It is, therefore, no surprise that most of us never really go beyond the comfort and convenience of the comfort zones we have created for ourselves. Every challenge and setback is viewed as the beginning of doom and most people make it their business to avoid any challenge or difficulty in their lives. Even if it means giving up on their dreams.

If you have often found yourself wondering why you simply cannot seem to find the mental strength to pursue your goals then you are not alone. Many people struggle with resilience and perseverance. Giving up often seems like the most convenient and easiest option yet by quitting every time things get hard; we end up missing out on life-changing opportunities.

For people who want the courage to go after their dreams and face their fears head-on, cultivating mental toughness is the way to do it. The ability to dedicate and commit yourself fully to purpose is one of the best ways to empower yourself to reach your goals. Think of how times you have given up or not even bothered to try because you could not muster up enough conviction to get you going. What if there was a way to discipline yourself to follow through on your dreams?

This book is meant for people who want to harness the power of their mental strength and use it to achieve their goals. It is geared towards helping people who are constantly giving up or getting distracted from their goals stay focused. *Mental Toughness* takes you through the common pitfalls that undermine your grit and resilience. It explores the connection between motivation and discipline in the achievement of goals and how these two aspects differ.

The majority of this book is devoted to exploring different strategies for improving mental strength and building the discipline that is required to follow through on your goals. The lessons contained in this book are meant for ordinary people who want to rise above their average existence and do something extraordinary with their lives.

If you are tired of missing opportunity after opportunity, tired of being stuck in a rut that you cannot seem to get out of and tired of seeing your dreams die, then this book, *Mental Toughness* is meant for you.

Chapter 1: Understanding Mental Toughness

Dave was not just having a bad day, if he was to be totally honest with himself, he was having a bad life. Sitting on the porch of the house that was about to be taken by the bank, he had no more lies to tell himself. He was a forty-two-year-old man who had just lost all his life savings, his life's work, and his wife. To top it all off, he was three weeks away from moving into his parent's basement.

Yes, the man voted 'most likely to succeed' among his small clique of college friends was now nothing more than a cliché. Dave had started at the top of the pile, as an associate in a top tier law firm in a city where up and coming lawyers were a dime a dozen. He had worked hard and his career had risen steadily and with it, his reputation as a man headed to the top.

Trudy, his ex-wife, had been attracted to the fast-rising star with glowing prospects. Their whirlwind courtship had culminated in a colorful wedding ceremony witnessed by their closest and dearest. Their marriage had been happy. They both loved the finer things in life and they had the bucks to live the good life, well, at least for a while. Trudy was as ambitious as she was beautiful. Dave had felt lucky to have found her. She had been the perfect yin to his yang. Trudy was an interior designer and she was one of the best. Dave had loved her ambition, and she in turn had loved his success.

The only thing he had failed to realize was that apparently, it was all she loved about him. When the shit hit the fan, and his spectacular fall from grace had started, Trudy was quick to disassociate herself from him. She filed for divorce quicker than he had filed for bankruptcy. He did not contest the separation, God knew he wanted to hold on to his marriage, but if there was one thing that he had learned through all this was that there was no use flogging a dead horse. So, he had signed the divorce papers and word about town was that Trudy was now happy in the arms of another lawyer, one who still had his job.

Dave still wondered at the speed at which his friends had deserted him in droves when the embezzlement case started. He had golfed with them, entertained them, and even given legal advice to some. Yet, when he had been wrongfully accused of embezzlement, no one, including his wife had stood by him. It was as if they thought that failure was infectious and that by staying close to him, they would somehow be tainted by Dave's mess. In hindsight he realized he had been naïve, rich people are notoriously fickle and if he was being honest, hadn't he done the same to his college friends?

When he had been on the up and up earlier in his career and his college friends were still struggling, Dave had found himself slowly growing distant from them. He did not understand why they kept whining instead of just getting their lives together like he had. They often accused him of being uppity and insensitive and when Dave finally got tired of feeling guilty for his success, he had ditched them. Now he was the one being ditched and he had to admit that karma was indeed a vengeful ice-cold bitch.

Sitting on his porch surrounded by the ruins of his life, Dave not for the first time wondered what had gone wrong. When did it start? What could he have done differently? Was it his fault? Bad luck? Was he too old to start all over? All these questions ran through his mind in a continuous loop and he had no answers for them, not a single one.

The Four Dimensions of Mental Toughness

It is easy to understand physical strength. This is because it is something that you can see and experience. When top athletes or bodybuilders want to increase their physical strength, they train tirelessly and work on their muscles until they build up their strength and physical endurance. But what about mental strength and toughness, what is it and more importantly can it be cultivated?

Mental toughness refers to the ability to persevere through difficult circumstances, bounce back from failure, and stay positive in situations that are far from ideal. It encompasses resilience, self-discipline, consistency, and commitment. Just like physical strength, mental toughness can be built by training your mind and pushing yourself constantly to deal with challenges and overcome failure.

Mentally tough people are not necessarily the most brilliant or intelligent people in the room. In actual fact, what sets mentally tough people apart from the average Joe is their ability to persevere, bounce back from failure, and stay committed to achieving their goals. This is why we often see that often the people who achieve extraordinary results are not the ones who excelled at school or have the most important academic accolades but rather the ones who refuse to give up.

Thomas Edison, Tom Cruise, Richard Branson, Anderson Cooper, and even the great Albert Einstein are people we have all heard off because they have made successes out of themselves in one way or another. However, what you may not know is that all these people also struggled with dyslexia early in life. Dyslexia which is a difficulty to read and write is a common learning disorder that affects the part of the brain that processes graphic symbols and sounds. What is interesting about this learning disorder is that despite having this condition, dyslexics have time and time again gone on to achieve extraordinary fetes in their lives. Which begs the question what is the link between dyslexia and success?

Well, there is no direct link between a learning disability and success. However, research has found that people who have to deal with failure and difficulty constantly early in life develop higher resilience than ordinary people. This means that people who have difficulty doing what other people can do easily such as reading and writing develop compensation learning.

Compensation learning is where someone makes up for what they cannot do by getting better at something else. This compensation learning is what has been found to make people with dyslexia likely to be successful later in life. Since they have to find ways to cope with their learning disability, they push themselves harder than other people, they get comfortable dealing with failure and as a result, they develop extraordinary resilience.

This extraordinary resilience is what gives people the mental strength to pursue their goals no matter how difficult the circumstances are. This mental toughness is born of the need to overcome failure and deal with whatever life throws your way. Mental strength goes beyond resilience to include self-discipline and the ability to stay committed to your goals.

The real test of mental toughness is not what you do when things are going your way but rather what you do when things are falling apart. When you are under pressure and on the brink of failure? Do you give up and run or do you keep going? Are you comfortable challenging yourself and pushing yourself out of your comfort zone? These are the kind of questions that point to how mentally strong you are.

Hope

If you go back to Dave's situation at the beginning of the chapter, what would you do if you were in Dave's shoes? Would you write yourself off or would you have enough hope to begin again? To have mental toughness, you must have hope. Hope that you can do better, hope that your situation can change, and hope that there is something better waiting on the other side.

When you reach a roadblock in your life and you feel that you have for all intents and purposes reached the very bottom of the barrel, you will only be able to get back up on your feet if you have hope. Hope is a positive expectation of what is to come. If you lose this positive expectation, then more often than not, you will often find yourself giving up easily because you cannot see beyond your current circumstances.

When hopelessness sets in, then the first thing to go is your resilience. To be able to bounce back from failure, you need to be able to expect that the situation can and will get better. This is why hope is one of the dimensions of mental toughness. People who are mentally strong always have an unwavering belief in themselves and they always know that there is something that can be done to overcome failure and difficulty.

Staying hopeful in situations where it seems like there is no way out is the first step in building mental resilience. If you lack self-belief then how can you pick yourself up and start again after failing? If Dave, for instance, can keep his self-belief-he will understand that just because he is going through a hard time, it does not mean he cannot get back on his feet. He will learn from his mistakes and start again wiser and stronger. Whether he has hope or not will determine what his next move will be. If he has hope, he will start again circumstances be-damned but if he has no hope, he will ultimately see his failure as a permanent situation and resign himself to his fate.

Hope is essentially the difference between where you are now and where you know you can be. It is the fuel that gives the power to pursue your goals and keep you moving forward because you understand that there is something better down the road if only you keep moving forward.

Confidence

Confidence just like hope is born from a strong belief in yourself. Confident people do not waste time counting the reasons why they cannot achieve their goals. Instead, they focus on their strengths and leverage them to get where they want to go. A confident person will see failure as a minor bump on the road and they will somehow find the inner reserves to keep them going.

Why is it that confidence appeals to so many people? Even in job interviews, candidates who appear more confident in themselves are more likely to get the job than those who do not. It is simply because confident people get things done. They are not afraid to take chances or take a risk because they believe in themselves and their abilities. This does not mean that confident people are always right or that they have no weaknesses, it means that they have the ability to overcome their fear and stay on course until they achieve their objectives.

Confidence is one of the key dimensions of mental strength. It gives you the ability to face down your fears and push yourself outside of your comfort zone. Think of the times when you have been reluctant to take on a challenge or pursue something difficult. Most of the time you will find that your hesitation is caused by a lack of confidence in your abilities. You will often talk yourself out of doing something when you do not believe you have what it takes or that you can face up to the competition.

To build your mental strength you must have confidence in yourself and your abilities. You must have enough self-belief to see beyond your weaknesses and trust your ability to overcome whatever challenge is in your way. if you truly think about it you will find that confidence is one half of mental toughness. Without it, you will not even have the guts to go after your dreams or try anything that challenges you.

Perseverance

You may have read the famous Harry Potter series by J.K Rowling. Even if you have not read about it, you have certainly heard about it. What you may not have heard about is that this famous author had her book rejected twelve times before it was finally published. When you think of successful people, it is easy to focus on their success and forget that they too had to go through a journey to get where they are.

If you were in the same shoes as J.K Rowling what are the chances that you would keep trying after twelve rejections? Chances are you would not because, for most people, one rejection is usually enough to discourage us from pursuing our dreams. J. K Rowling persevered through failure after failure until she finally got what she wanted. This kind of perseverance is one of the key ingredients that will always set apart people who achieve extraordinary fetes from others.

Perseverance is the determination to see your dreams come to life no matter what it takes. People who are mentally strong do not have giving up as an option. They fail and get rejected just like everybody else, but unlike other people, they get up time and time again. This perseverance is what it means to understand that failure is part and parcel of getting to success. If you always set out to achieve your goals but only if things go your way, then the probability is you will give up on more goals than you will pursue.

Without perseverance, any obstacles in your path will seem like the end of the road. Perseverance is what helps you stay committed and consistent in pursuing your goal. Without perseverance, you cannot achieve mental toughness and you will always give up when things get tough.

Resilience

In the book Who Moved my Cheese? The author uses the analogy of mice to explain how some people find it difficult to adapt to change and move on. One of the dimensions of mental toughness is the ability not just to bounce back from failure but also to reinvent yourself and adapt to the situation.

If you cannot adapt to situations as they evolve you will always be stuck in a rut watching life pass you buy. You cannot always use the same attitudes, beliefs, methods, and emotions you have always used if you hope to achieve things you have never achieved. The ability to change and reinvent yourself is crucial for mental strength. Think of it this way, if you are driving to a destination and it is blocked for one reason or another, will you turn back and go home or look for a different route?

Resilience gives you the ability to recognize that if one thing is not working, you can always try something else. It opens up your mind and helps you shed self-limiting beliefs and embrace new perspectives that equip you to seize new opportunities.

In the book Who Moved my Cheese, there were two types of mice. When the cheese in the maze is no longer where it used to be, Scurry and Sniff decided to look for cheese in other parts of the maze. In contrast, the other mice, Hem and Hall, were dismayed to find the cheese had moved and stayed in the same spot hoping that the cheese will return. Scurry and Sniff found new cheese elsewhere in the maze even as the other mice wasted time complaining and waiting for the cheese to come back.

Who would you be in this scenario? Are you the kind of person who keeps doing the same thing over and over and expecting different results? Or are you the kind of person who adapts to the situation and finds ways to adjust? Mentally tough people accept change, adapt to it, and keep moving. Instead of dwelling on how the circumstances are no longer in their favor, resilient people commit their energy to coping with the new situation and making it favorable.

To cultivate mental toughness, resilience is one of the traits you will have to build in yourself. With resilience, change and setbacks will no longer be daunting but you will start to see them as opportunities to try something new and reinvent yourself.

The Link Between Mental Toughness & Success

Everybody has their own definition of success. For some success is being at the top in terms of their careers, for others, it has to do with all-round fulfillment in their lives and for some, it is about being better than the person you were yesterday. Whatever your definition of success is, the one thing most people will agree on is that it does not come easy. You have to toil, work, and dedicate yourself tirelessly in order to achieve your goals.

The link between mental toughness and success is that mental toughness is what helps you persevere, remain consistent, and refuse to give up on your goals. It is the difference between giving up after the first try and trying thirteen times if that is what it takes to reach your goal. Without mental toughness, your life will become about reaching for the low hanging fruit. In this zone, you will settle for the things that you can get as opposed to fighting for things that you know you deserve.

You will settle for that low paying job because you do not have the guts to after the job that you really want. You will never ask the girl of your dreams out because you are afraid of being shot down and you will settle in so many other ways just to avoid the risk of failure. Living a life of settling is what most people do when they do not have the mental strength to go after what they really want. They complain and whine about their lives, yet they never take any steps to change their outcomes or chase their dreams.

In contrast, for people who are mentally tough, the only acceptable result is what they want. They are passionate about their goals and do not let failure, opposition, or fatigue stand in their way. They rise up again and again and keep trying until they get it right. Ultimately this grit and sheer endurance are what make mental toughness a prerequisite for success.

If you have been struggling with reaching your goals or seeing your plans through to the end, then mental toughness could be the missing link. It is the bridge between where you are now and where you need to go. Think of all the times you have set out to do something and then given up halfway when things got tough. What if you had seen it through? What if you had refused to surrender? Would your life be different because of it? Would you be a better person because of the experience?

No matter which way you slice it, you need resilience and you need grit to succeed. From sportsmen to business executives, to family men or women and even students, to really achieve the extraordinary, you have to be mentally strong. Like it or not, life will always have challenges, difficulties, and setbacks to overcome. If you can muster up the mental strength to deal with these challenges then success, whichever way you define it, will only be a matter of time.

Are You Mentally Tough?

Here is a simple quiz to help you gauge your level of mental toughness

1. Do you remain calm in a crisis and focus on fixing the problem?
2. Do you have a positive outlook even when things are not going according to plan?
3. Do you function well in new environments and adapt quickly to change?
4. Do you thrive on challenges and often sign up for new opportunities or tasks that challenge you?
5. Do you make bold choices and often do things other people consider risky?

6. Are you good at managing stress and finding ways to keep yourself emotionally balanced?
7. Are you confident in your abilities and not afraid to fail?
8. Are you comfortable asking for help when you are stuck?
9. Do you like to try new things and push your own boundaries?

➢ If you answered mostly yes to these questions it indicates that you are mentally tough and are not afraid to take on challenges.
➢ If you had an equal number of yes's and no's, it indicates that you are mentally tough but can on occasion give in to self-doubt.
➢ If you answered mostly no's, it indicates that you have not built up resilience and so you avoid situations that challenge or push you out of your comfort zone.

Chapter 2: The Spartan Way

If you know the enemy and know yourself, you need not fear the result of a hundred battles - Sun Tzu, The Art of War

In a world where instant gratification is king, grit and resilience are becoming increasingly elusive traits. Human beings have made it their business to seek comfort and security at any cost. Think of all the nifty gadgets that you have in your life to make your life easier. The phone that wakes you up in the morning, the app that tells you when to eat or when to work out, the GPS that tells you which is the shortest route and everything else that you simply "cannot live without".

Conveniences are good, technology is great and there is nothing wrong with wanting to be comfortable and secure. This need for comfort and security however comes at a cost. The more comfortable you get, the more comfort you seek and on and on it goes. Research has actually found that on average, stress levels are significantly higher now than they were ten or even twenty years ago. Which begs the question, if we have so many creature comforts, devices, and a host of other things dedicated to making our lives easier, why are we the most miserable generation?

The truth is that, increasingly, we have trained ourselves to put comfort and convenience above all else. You have been conditioned to think that the easiest way is the best way out. So little by little your brain becomes accustomed to seeking comfort and gratification while steering a path around anything that is challenging, difficult, or uncomfortable.

Water in a stream, electricity and even Google maps all take the path of least resistance. So does the human brain. The things we do the most become the things that we are most likely to repeat simply because our brain is naturally wired to follow the neural pathways that we have reinforced over time. This is how habits become ingrained patterns of behavior.

The more you do something the more entrenched the neural pathway for that particular activity becomes in your brain. You may not realize it but most of the habits you have created over time are much deeper than just surface characteristics. Habits alter the way your brain works and predispose you to behave and think in predictable patterns.

Most people who constantly have problems in their careers, in relationships, or even just staying focused have one thing in common. They will tell you that they often feel that their life is more or less a case of *same shit different day*. Their lives seem to unfold in predictable patterns and they end up facing the same challenges over and over. Ultimately, they get stuck in a rut because they simply have no idea why their life is going round in circles.

The Dog You Feed

Our lives are a series of choices. From the time your feet hit the ground in the morning, you are always choosing. What to wear, what to have for breakfast, whether to go to the gym and everything else that you will do. More often than not you will make these choices without really stopping to think about it because these are mundane everyday things that are pretty much routine.

But what happens when it comes to really big life decisions? Like whether to go for that promotion at work, whether to ask that person you really like out or whether to quit your job and start a business. These bigger choices come with greater consequences and this is where most people become caught up in their fears and insecurities.

When you are in a situation where you have to pick one of two paths. What are you most likely to do? Are your decisions driven by the fear of uncertainty or are you comfortable challenging yourself? If you have made your life all about comfort and security, chances are every decision you make will be based on what is the least challenging option or what option carries the lowest risk. This is because for you the only acceptable choice is anything that lets you stay in your comfort zone and does not challenge your identity.

Let's consider two people working in the same organization. Mark and James work in the same department in a law firm where there is an opening for a manager. Mark wants the job but he does not want to talk to his boss about it because he is afraid that he may not get the job so he chooses to not make a move. On the other hand, when James learns that there is an opening in his department, he puts together a presentation showing why he is the best man for the job and makes his case to the boss.

In this scenario, these two people have access to the same opportunity. One of them is afraid to fail so he decides to do nothing while the other may very well be afraid but chooses to put himself out there all the same. Now there is no guarantee that

James will get the job simply because he asked for it, but he has a better chance of getting it than Mark who did not even try. Chances are, even if he does not get this particular promotion, James will ultimately go further in his career because he is not afraid to take a chance or seize an opportunity.

In every challenging situation, there will always be two options, you can give in to your fear or you can take a chance and seize the opportunity before you. If you had two dogs, naturally if you feed one more than the other it becomes the bigger and more dominant dog. In this case, if one dog is fear and the other is take a chance, the more often you feed fear and neglect take a chance, the stronger fear becomes, and naturally, the weaker take a chance gets.

This is the simple analogy of the dog that you choose to feed. Before you make a decision ask yourself, which dog did I feed today? Did I feed fear or did I feed take a chance? The more you look at your choices not just as short-term decisions but as something that you have to live with long term, the easier it becomes to make the right decision.

Think of what your decision will mean a year or five down the line. Will you have the job of your dreams because you took a chance or will you still be pushing paper at your desk because you were too scared to try? Will you have married the girl of your dreams or will you still be the lonely guy who is home alone every Friday night? A minute of giving in to fear can cost you for far much longer than you bargained for.

The reason your life seems to unfold in familiar patterns is that given the same situation you will often make the same choice. Ultimately our choices have less to do with the external circumstances than they have to do with who we are. If we go back to the example of Mark and James, if another opportunity was to arise, they will both likely have the same reaction to it. James will go for it because he has made a habit of taking chances and Mark will most likely let the opportunity pass because he is afraid of the possible outcome.

This is where the problem becomes more than just a missed opportunity and morphs into a wasted life. When you make a habit of shying away from challenging or difficult situations then you will pretty much spend your life picking the low hanging fruit. Since you do not want to stretch and make yourself uncomfortable you will make a habit of settling and accepting things that you can easily change. You will attribute the bad experiences, missed opportunities, and setbacks in your life to bad luck, fate, or destiny never realizing that all along it is you who chose to feed the wrong dog.

Mental toughness is the ability to get past your doubts, fears, and self-limiting beliefs and pursue your goals. It means having dogged endurance, passion, and perseverance that drives you to achieve your goals without letting fear or lack of focus get in your way. Mentally tough people cultivate discipline, focus, and resilience in themselves. They are persistent in the pursuit of their dreams and are not afraid of competition, or unfavorable circumstances.

When you are mentally tough your belief and confidence are in your own abilities. Your strength is in who you are and not what the circumstances are or who the competition is. This mindset is what made the Spartans of ancient Greece one of the most formidable forces in history. Their strength was not in their numbers; in fact, they often fought enemies with larger armies. Their success was built on discipline, resilience, grit, and the determination to win.

Spartans were not intimidated by how many soldiers their enemies had. They were not concerned about whether the odds were in the favor. Their mission was to win, and surrender and defeat were never an option. This ultimately was the key to their success. Spartans were dedicated to their goal and their discipline and focus were their most powerful weapons against their enemies.

You may not be going into battle with a shield and a sword like the Spartans of old. However, every single day you make choices whether to surrender or persist, to falter or to stay focused and whether to believe in yourself or fear the circumstances and the competition. Ultimately these are the choices that shape who you are and determine whether or not you will live the life that you have always wanted.

The Fear of Uncertainty

Mental toughness is built on a foundation of being comfortable with uncertainty and a willingness to challenge yourself. Think of all the times you have let an opportunity pass you by. When you chose to go for the job you thought you could get rather than the one that you really wanted. When you decided not to go back to college because you thought you would never graduate or when you decided not to pursue that business idea because it would mean taking a chance.

Whatever it is that you passed on, when you stop to think about most of the missed opportunities in your life, you will realize that most of the time what stops you from going for what you want is the fear of uncertainty. *What if I fail? What if I am not good enough? What if there is a better candidate? What If she doesn't like me?* There is an infinite number of what-ifs that can stop you from going after what you want.

Fear is one of the biggest motivators known to man. It is the reason that most people remain stuck in situations that are less than ideal. They choose to remain within their comfort zone because their fear of the unknown is greater than their passion or their goals. You will find people who are constantly complaining about their lives, their jobs, their relationships or financial situations and so many other aspects of their lives that they have the power to change. So why do we stay in these situations and keep complaining?

Most of the battles we lose are the ones we lost on the inside long before they were fought on the outside. You talk yourself out of doing things every day because you are afraid of what the outcome will be or how it will change your life. It is funny how we fear change and yearn for it at the same time. You want a better life but you would rather not do something different or choose something that is outside the norm. How can you get different results doing the same things over and over?

The more afraid you are of the unknown the more likely you are to stay in a rut. That is why cultivating mental toughness is so important. Mental toughness teaches you to embrace uncertainty and accept that failure is an inevitable part of success. When you take your fear out of the equation, what else is holding you back from going after what you want? Nothing. Behind all our excuses, is fear, fear of failure, fear of change, and so many other fears.

Once these fears are dispelled then the rest of the excuses fall like dominoes and the path to your goal becomes clear.

When the fear of uncertainty is enough to keep you from pursuing your dreams, it means that your commitment and dedication to the goal are not strong enough. When you are passionate about what you want, even when you are not sure of the outcome you are willing to take a chance because the probability of success is enough to motivate you. This is why passion and commitment are an integral part of mental toughness. If you have no real passion and dedication to your goals, then you will easily give up at the first sign of difficulty or trouble. Set goals that are meaningful to you and that are worth fighting for.

Comfort in Victimhood

People who lack mental toughness will often be comfortable in the role of the victim. If you often find yourself looking for scapegoats for why things went wrong or why your life is not going the way it should then you probably find comfort in victimhood. Now in normal circumstances, there is nothing good about being about a victim. When you are a victim it means you are powerless and at the mercy of your circumstances or other people. So why do so many people play the victim in their own lives?

Well, for starters playing the victim absolves you from taking the responsibility for your life and for your missteps. When it is always someone else's fault and not your own, then you still get to feel good about yourself even when things go wrong. Another reason why it is so easy to fall into the role of the victim is that when you are the victim you do not have to look at your own shortcomings. You can blame it on others, blame it on your circumstances but never feel the need to own the situation.

If you fall into this trap, you will often find yourself saying things like, *if only my boss wasn't so mean I would be better at my job, or my relationship would have worked if my partner was more understanding or I would have passed the test if I had more time...and many more excuses.* People who find comfort in victimhood have an excuse for every season and a season for every excuse. The fault always lies elsewhere and so their life is a never-ending cycle of passing the buck. Of course, with this kind of mindset, it is almost impossible to reach your goals.

Mental toughness teaches you that you are the author of your fate, not the circumstances, and certainly not the competition. This is what the Spartans believed in. They did not leave the outcome of their battles to the circumstances or to the enemy. Every step of the way, they made sure that they were in charge of their own outcome. They created the circumstances they wanted by having a plan and seeing it through no matter what.

When you are simply riding the wave without a clear goal in mind or a particular purpose then more often than not you live life in a reactive role. You react to the things that are happening around you, so naturally, you do not have much control over what happens in your life. Reactive people base their actions on what other people do or what the situation is. In contrast, people who are mentally tough create the circumstances and let other people react to them. That is the main difference between being a victim and being in control of your life.

To cultivate mental toughness, you have to get brutally honest with yourself. What are you blaming other people for that is really your own doing? When you identify your blind spots, you have a better chance of coming out of that rut you are stuck in than if you spend your energy and time looking for scapegoats.

At the end of the day, the only person responsible for your life is you. Even the people who love you and care for you cannot change your outcomes for you. Mental toughness is an inside job that starts with the ability to acknowledge where you are in life, accepting responsibility for your own life, and taking the reins for your future firmly in your hands.

Nothing Happens Until You Move

When we think of courage, it is often in association with people who are fearless or extraordinary in some way. The truth is courage, just like fear is a habit that can be created. If we go back to the legend of the Spartans, their courage was not based on emotion but rather on their discipline. Their preparation before battle, their dedication to their course, and their commitment to winning are what gave them courage, not a lack of fear of the enemy.

Emotions drive most of our decisions. You often do things because they feel right or because they make you happy. These emotional decisions are the reason why it is so hard to leave your comfort zone. You want to feel safe and secure so you choose the path that is not challenging or difficult. Often this means staying where you are and missing out on opportunities because they make you feel threatened in some way.

You cannot develop mental toughness unless you first learn how to regulate your emotions. The courage of the Spartans was not born of feeling, but discipline and having a goal that was bigger than their emotions. When you think of courage stop waiting for the day when you will not feel afraid or scared. That day may never come because emotions are a natural part of the human experience. Courage is not the absence of fear altogether but rather the willingness to feel the fear but do what needs to be done anyway.

Think of performers who suffer from stage fright. They experience anxiety and nerve-wracking fear before a performance but once they get on stage and feel the energy of the crowd the fear melts away. The simple reason for this is that the only way to beat fear is by acting. Fear goes hand in hand with inaction. The more you are paralyzed by fear, the bigger the fear becomes. On the contrary, when you make a move, the fear gradually dissipates. When you act, you start to realize, *this isn't so bad, I can do this*.

If you are tired of being held captive by fear, seeing opportunities pass you by, and missing out on the life you know you can have, it starts with action. Make a move.

Chapter 3: The Psychology of Willpower, Motivation, and Discipline

Getting up every day to go to the gym, setting aside time for studying every day, rehearsing daily for a show or performance, or training each day for a sports event. What do all these things have in common? They all require commitment and discipline. The truth is, you will not always feel like working out, or studying or doing anything productive, somedays you will just want to do the bare minimum. So, what will keep you going when willpower and motivation fail you?

Mentally tough people understand something that most people do not. Motivation and willpower are certainly good to have but they come in waves. They are emotions and just like any other emotions they come and go depending on the circumstances, your environment, and a host of other factors. In essence, your motivation is not always up to you. Sometimes someone may say something discouraging and make you feel worthless or you may be facing circumstances that simply take the wind out of your sails.

What this means if you are relying on willpower and motivation alone. You will have a problem being consistent. One day you are raring to go, the next it's all you can do to get out of bed. This is what happens when your productivity is influenced by your emotions. How often have you started something only to lose steam halfway through it and give it up altogether? Think of people who start every year with grand ideas of turning their life around. They follow through on their resolutions until somewhere in mid-January then gradually start to fall back to old patterns of behavior.

The people who have cultivated mental toughness realize that motivation is a feeling, it comes and goes. So, they do not make it the main reason behind what they do. Instead, they invest in plans, schedules, and habits. They understand that consistency and self-discipline are the only tools that will keep you on track no matter what your mood is or what the circumstances are.

When you prioritize habits and action plans over motivation and willpower, you are no longer going on emotions alone. Self-discipline ties you to certain actions regardless of what frame of mind you are in. When you create habits and action plans, every day you wake up knowing what you have to do, why you have to do it and when it needs to be done. This ultimately is more beneficial when it comes to productivity than motivation will ever be.

Many times, when you are waiting around for motivation or inspiration you end up wasting valuable time. You end up procrastinating and putting off important decisions and tasks because you are not in the right frame of mind. Mentally tough people realize that if they establish daily habits, create schedules for themselves and stay focused on the goal, they have a better chance of success than someone who just sits back waiting for a dose of motivation or inspiration.

Think of pro-athletes. They practice every day without fail. The star player of the team will show up for practice just like the weaker players will. They do not tell the more talented players to sit at home and wait for game-day since they are already good. This is because the universal truth that practice makes perfect applies to all. It does not matter how good you are at something, or how talented you are, if you are not consistent and disciplined, sooner or later things will start to go south.

Let's consider writers for a moment. They bring words to life and create content for other people to enjoy. If on one hand, you have a writer who only writes when they feel motivated and on the other, you have a writer who has a schedule where they write at least two thousand words per day, who is likely to be more productive? Undoubtedly the writer with the schedule will be more productive because he is not driven by moods or emotions. He has a plan of action and he follows it consistently every day.

The reason many people fail to achieve their goals is not that they do know what they want but rather because they do not have a plan of action. You want a new job, but what are you doing about it? You want better grades, but how are you changing your study routine? You want a healthier body, but what changes have you made? Without a plan, you will simply be going on motivation and willpower. As soon as the motivation starts to wane you give up and revert back to default settings.

Motivation is not a plan and it certainly is not consistent. If that is all you are banking on then your chances of achieving your goals are slim to none. Why do yo-yo dieters always end up putting back on all the weight they had lost? It is simply because they focus on the result instead of investing in the process. Instead of cultivating self-discipline and perseverance, yo-yo dieters rely on motivation and willpower. Ultimately when the motivation fizzles out, they find themselves right where they started. They jump to the next fad diet not realizing that it is not the diet that needs to change but rather their approach.

Mental toughness is about taking deliberate steps to make your dreams come true. You do not wait for inspiration to hit, or for the moment to feel right, you simply start and make daily habits that then become ingrained into your daily life. The short story is, without self-discipline and consistency, motivation and willpower will only take you so far.

Self- Awareness

There is no escaping yourself. Everywhere you go, well, there you are. This may sound pretty inane but it is probably one of the most important realizations you will make in your life. Your attitude, your beliefs, your values, and your emotional baggage follow you around in every situation. They are the invisible coat you put on each day before you go out to face the world. These beliefs, attitudes, and values influence how you see yourself, how you see others, and how you approach challenges and opportunities.

Do you know of a person who goes from one bad relationship to another? Every relationship they get into seems to end the same way? Or someone who always hits a plateau at work no matter how many times they switch jobs. They always think the next opportunity will be their breakthrough only to end up in the same exact situation they were trying to escape.

These situations, where life seems to be unfolding in similar patterns repeatedly, occur because of the baggage you carry around with you. If you behave the same way in your current relationship that you did in your last one, why would the outcome be any different? If you work in the same way you have always done why would your boss suddenly notice you? Recognizing the role that we play in the way circumstances unfold around us is crucial in breaking cycles of dysfunction, broken dreams, and unhappiness. Find the enemy within before you look for the one on the outside.

If you are blind to your own self-limiting beliefs, you will never conquer your demons. You will always be fighting the same problems in the same way and wondering why your life is going round in circles. Self-awareness is the only way to realize how we sabotage our own success.

How often do you talk yourself out of doing things that you know might be good for you? You tell yourself; *I don't have the experience there is no way I would get a better job,* or *I am too fat, it is too late to start exercising,* or *I will never get into college why bother studying?* Are you paying attention to your internal dialogue? What do you say to yourself, are you your own worst critique or are you cheering yourself on?

Self -sabotage is so difficult to beat because it is intrinsically tied to who we think we are, our self-esteem, and our identity. You will often hear people say things, like, *Oh I do not like to socialize, that's just the way I am wired,* or *I am just really bad at Math, there is no way I am passing that test.* When you box yourself into a certain identity then effectively you stop yourself from even trying. The more you do it, the more limited your opportunities become because your mind is closed to things that do not feel comfortable or familiar to you.

To become mentally tough, you need to understand that your own beliefs are the biggest hindrance to your success. You have to stop seeking ways to reinforce your beliefs and instead embrace things that make you question the identity you have created for yourself.

For instance, if you hate socializing, make it a point to go out every weekend. Do it every weekend without fail until it becomes a habit. It may be hard at first but the more you do it, you will start to realize that there is really nothing daunting about it. It is just a different experience that you are fully capable of handling. The point here is to challenge who you think you are by doing something you would never do. Even if you never really get to like it, you will learn how to cope with uncomfortable situations and grow in the process.

Remember we learn the most when we push ourselves outside of our comfort zones. Do not get so caught up in sticking to an image you have created for yourself that you miss out on opportunities that have the power to change your life. If you think about it, most of the labels you have put on yourself are simply shields you have developed to protect yourself and to avoid feeling vulnerable.

You tell yourself you are underqualified so that you do not have to take a chance on asking for a raise or you tell yourself you are too fat so that you do not have to challenge yourself by working out. All these little lies we tell ourselves are all about holding on to the identities we have created for ourselves. They make you feel safe because you do not have to push your boundaries or step out of your comfort zone. You can simply sit back and say, *that's not my thing, no point in trying*.

The more self-aware you become the easier it will be to bust the self-limiting beliefs and stop self-sabotaging. Before you make a decision, ask yourself, *why am I choosing this instead of the other? Am I afraid to challenge myself?* By questioning your motives, emotions, and triggers you will start to unravel all the little ways in which you derail your progress.

The David Vs Goliath Complex

David was a little shepherd boy who dared to take on a mammoth Philistine warrior even when seasoned soldiers would not. When soldiers from his side looked across the battlefield at the huge enemy on the other side, all they saw was a beast that could not be beaten. So, they did not even try, after all the price would have been their own lives.

Along comes this teenage shepherd boy who has never done anything but herd sheep in his life. However, unlike the soldiers from his side, he does not know enough to be scared. In fact, he does not know much about the mammoth Philistine that has intimidated seasoned soldiers into inaction. All David knows, is that he is pretty good with a slingshot. He also knows that the mammoth Philistine is such a big target that it would be hard not to hit him. So, David takes his shot, and his stones hit home just like he knew they would.

When faced with a challenge most people tend to focus on how big it is, or why its impossible to overcome. Very few people take the David approach of focusing inward and finding their inner strength. In the natural scheme of things, a teenage shepherd boy has no real chance against a battle-hardened soldier but he can skew the odds in his favor by facing the opponent on his own terms. David used what he knew to win a battle no one else would have because they could not see past the size of the challenge.

David saw the size of the challenge as an advantage, Goliath was so big that he made the perfect target. You do not have to be a Christian to understand the lesson in David and Goliath. It simply teaches us to stop focusing on the competition and instead focus on what our own strengths are and how we can leverage them to turn the situation in our favor. This principle is the same one that the Spartans of ancient Greece used. They did not waste time wondering how many soldiers the enemy had, they focused all their energy on their discipline, their own strategy, and how to win.

If every time you are faced with a challenge, your mind immediately goes to why it cannot be done then do not be surprised if you are constantly giving up. If you have no belief or faith in your abilities then every challenge will seem like an insurmountable mountain. You have to overcome your fears and doubts to be able to go after what you want. This is why you cannot have mental toughness without resilience or perseverance. If you always quit at the first sign of trouble or difficulty, it is time to turn your focus from the problems and focus on your strengths.

Stop waiting for the right moment, or for the odds to turn in your favor. We create our own luck by making consistent, strides towards our goals and pushing ourselves until we achieve them. Invest in consistent actions and habits that bring you closer to your goals and stop waiting for inspiration or motivation. If they come along, well and good, but if they do not you will have your discipline and habits to keep you on the right path.

Start by identifying what you want. Do you want a better job? Do you want to lose that extra weight? Do you want to meet someone and get married? Whatever it is you are aiming for, once you have a clear goal then you can identify what you need to do every day to achieve it. If for instance, your goal is to get a better job, you can set aside an hour or two each day to send out applications to suitable companies. Do this every day until you get an interview. It will only be a matter of time before you get a yes.

The same principle of discipline and consistency applies if your goal is getting into shape. Have a daily workout schedule that you stick to each day. Train yourself to eat healthy by making a conscious effort daily to avoid junk food. When you discipline yourself by creating a schedule and tying yourself to deliberate and specific actions, you are no longer depending on moods or inspiration to get you what you want.

When you create a plan and follow through on it, you are effectively taking control of your outcome and making a decision to be in charge of what happens in your life.

Ditching Bad Habits

Habits are the things that keep you tied to your past. Until you ditch your old habits then, you have no chance of changing your life. Habits determine who you are, what you can achieve, and even how far you will get in life. Your ability to achieve mental toughness is intrinsically tied to your ability to ditch old habits and create new ones.

The one mistake that people keep making over and over is waiting for motivation to get started. Why do you need to wait until new years to make that resolution? why will you start eating healthy on Monday not today? When you delay action, you lose time, you lose motivation and ultimately you lose your discipline. This Monday becomes next Monday and everything challenging is pushed to a "tomorrow" that never comes.

People who achieve greatness do not wait for motivation to swoop in and sweep them off their feet. Instead, they commit to a process that requires them to take deliberate action today, not tomorrow or the day after. The one thing that habits, both good and bad have in common is consistency. You do not develop an addiction overnight. You abuse a substance every day for an extended period of time until it becomes something you cannot live without. In much the same way, to ditch bad habits and create new ones, you have to do something consistently for an extended period of time until it becomes a way of life. Why would you expect that years of bad eating habits can be changed by a week of dieting? Of course, it is impossible, and yet so many people get discouraged and give up the minute they do not see change. That is why banking on your motivation to achieve your goals can be treacherous.

When you rely on self-discipline and habits instead of will power you give yourself a better chance at success because you remove emotions from the equation. You hold yourself accountable to certain tasks and actions each day and these become your new habits. When you are motivated, you are only driven by the results. However, when you are self-disciplined you are more interested in the process so you focus more on what you need to do. This mentality of investing in the process is what will help you to ditch old habits and create new ones.

Start by looking at the habits that you want to change. Are you slacking off at work? Is your relationship on the verge of falling apart because you make no time for it? Are you flunking out of school because you rarely study? Whatever it is that is holding you back from achieving your goals, identify it, and acknowledge it. Then ask yourself what you can do each day, not once in a while, but each day to turn the situation around.

Once you have identified which area of your life you want to change. Create a schedule. This schedule involves taking a deliberate action towards your goals every day. This could be making sure you have worked on everything in your in-tray at work every day without fail, it could be working out daily for half an hour at a particular time or setting aside two hours each day to study. Whatever action that you choose to make part of your schedule should be tied to the bad habit you want to ditch.

Once you have a schedule, make it a point to follow it each day until it becomes second nature. Do not stop for the weather, or to take a break, or any other excuse you have used in the past to give yourself permission to quit. Cultivate self-discipline by sticking to the schedule you have created no matter what.

To make the change easier, focus on making small changes rather than making a full 180-degree turn. Do not go to extremes like deciding that you will spend three hours at the gym daily when you have never worked out a day in your life. Make sensible but deliberate changes that will help you stay on track. Remember that motivation and willpower are good things to have but they are focused on results. You can only achieve real change if you invest in the process and that ultimately is what self-discipline is all about.

Chapter 4: Grit and Resilience

Thomas Edison failed 1000 times before he invented the light bulb. J K Rowling's Harry Potter was rejected 12 times before it was finally published. Henry Ford faced bankruptcy five times before he put Ford on the world map. When we look at these extraordinary people who have achieved greatness, we only see the result but not the journey. You may never know what it took someone to get where they are today because it is human nature to prioritize the result over the process.

We often assume that some people are so successful because they have outstanding brilliance or talent. Yet, the truth is that it is not the talent or the brilliance that makes them achieve greatness but rather their unwillingness to quit or surrender. Imagine the kind of mindset that it takes to be rejected twelve times and still try for the thirteenth. That is the secret behind people who achieve greatness. Their extraordinary resilience and perseverance in situations when anyone else would simply call it quits.

A lot of people are talented and many are skilled yet few make it to the very top. This is because true greatness comes at a price that few of us, no matter how talented are willing to pay; perseverance. Most people will never get to be rejected twelve times for the simple reason that they will never try that many times at anything. You may try twice or even thrice but for most people failing once is usually enough reason to give up. Perseverance is a skill very few people muster because it is not easy, or quick or convenient.

What makes these people that we celebrate everyday outstanding is not that they are more talented or more skilled than everyone else. It is their determination to succeed and the unwillingness to surrender that sets them apart from the average Joe or Jane.

Grit is about getting comfortable with failure and accepting it as a normal part of the process that leads to success. People who are willing to take extraordinary chances are those who are not daunted by the possibility of failure. They are not interested in playing it safe or sitting by the edge of the pool. They dive in again and again until they get what they want. This willingness and ability to keep trying time and time again is what defines mental strength.

When you have failed time and time again but you do not accept defeat as an option, then you have achieved mental toughness. Think for a minute, what do you do when you are rejected? When you are under pressure and running out of options how do you react? Do you fold and give up or do you get up and try again? Extraordinary things are only achieved through extraordinary resilience and perseverance. That is why there are only a few amongst us who will ever achieve greatness.

The No-Surrender Mindset

Actor Will Smith was once asked how he manages to keep his marriage together in an industry where divorce is the norm. He answered that divorce was never an option for him and his wife. So, once it was off the table they had to work on their issues and come to a solution no matter what. In many ways, this explains the no-surrender mindset. What happens when giving up is not an option? Naturally, you focus on fixing the situation because that is the only option you have.

Often, we sabotage ourselves by giving ourselves an easy way out in case things do not work out. How many times do you actually plan to fail in advance? Have you ever told yourself, *in case it does not work out, I will do this instead?* What if in this same scenario instead of making failure an option you took the no surrender mindset and said, *in case it does not work, I will keep trying until it does.* When you know that quitting is not an option then all your focus is on how to get it done.

The thing about quitting is that if you do it often enough, it becomes a habit. The more you give up, the easier it gets to do the next time. That is why you will find some people try one thing after another without ever seeing anything through. Not because they do not have the talent or the skills required, but rather because they have made a habit out of quitting. When the going gets tough, the only option they see is quitting because they have trained themselves to shy away from adversity or difficulty.

The path of least resistance will always be the easiest one to take so if you have made a habit out of giving up, you will always find a reason why something is too hard or too difficult. You will talk yourself out of seizing opportunities because you are not willing to accept challenges as an integral part of success. You want the end result but you are not ready to go through the process that gives you the results. So, you waste time procrastinating and finding excuses for not doing what you should be doing.

To build your mental toughness, you have to be disciplined enough to invest in the process to get the results. Stop looking for shortcuts and commit to doing the work. This is what the no-surrender mindset is about. It is about the relentless pursuit of your goal even through difficulty and unfavorable conditions. If you are only willing to do things when they are easy or not too challenging then you will always be stuck in the same place wondering why your goals are always out of reach.

Perseverance starts with passion and commitment. The goals you set for yourself should be so important that nothing can deter you from pursuing them. Your goals should be the things that you see in your mind the first thing when you wake up and the last thing when you go to sleep. They should be things that you are passionate about.

One common mistake that people make is setting goals that hold no true meaning for them. You want to do something because it is important to someone else, or because you feel you should but not because it is important to you. With this kind of goal, you will always find it difficult to persevere. You can only be committed and driven when what you are working towards is truly important to you.

Find out what it is that you really want in life. Forget what other people want you to do or expect you to do, and focus on what it is that you want for yourself. List down your goals and the things that you want in your life. These could be financial goals, career goals, or even relationship goals. Whatever it is that you want, identify it, and visualize it. See yourself with those things that you want and imagine how it will feel when you finally achieve your goals.

When you visualize your goals, you make them into something tangible. That is why people use vision boards to remind themselves of what they are shooting for. There is something powerful about actually seeing what you could become if you committed to your goal.

Once you have set clear and meaningful goals for yourself, you can then focus your time and energy on the process of achieving them. Always keep your eye on the ball. When things get tough or when someone discourages you or even when you start to have doubts, remind yourself of what you are working towards and why it is important.

Go beyond just waiting for motivation or inspiration to strike. Invest in your goals by building habits and creating schedules that tie you to doing deliberate things each day to get to where you want to go. Having a goal will only be significant if you are taking steps towards it. If you simply have a goal but no plan on how to achieve it, then that is just wishful thinking.

Make yourself responsible for your life and your outcomes. Forget fate, or luck, or destiny. Whatever it is that you want out of life make it your business to make it happen. People with a no-surrender mindset understand that they must be in control of themselves in order to get what they want. They cannot wait for things to happen and react to them. They have to be proactive and keep the ball rolling.

Ultimately the no-surrender mindset is built on the principle of not giving up. Remove quitting from your list of options and start again. Not once, not twice, but as many times as it takes to get it done.

Disrupting Yourself

Insanity is often described as doing the same thing over and over and expecting different results. How is your belief system, attitude, and the image you have created for yourself working for you? Are you where you should be? Do you feel that you are on the right path? If you are unhappy, why are you accepting the situation instead of doing something about it?

Resilience is not just about being able to bounce back from failure but also being capable of reinventing yourself. Disrupting yourself means stripping away all the labels and attitudes you have covered yourself in and starting afresh. When your pen breaks, would you still keep trying to write with it? Of course not, because it is broken and not serving any purpose. So why are you holding on to beliefs, attitudes, and emotions that are not getting you anywhere?

For many people when they face difficulties, they always want to change the situation. You want to change jobs because your boss is a bully, or you want to change your major because what you are doing is too hard, or you want to change your diet because it is not working and you want to try another. In all these cases it probably never occurs to you to think about changing yourself instead of the situation. Why? Because it is always easier to try to change others than it is to change ourselves.

When you have lived with an identity for so long, change becomes so difficult that you never look inwards for your solution. In your mind, it is always the situation or the other person that needs to change. This explains why people who lack mental strength often end up playing the victim role in their lives. They stubbornly hold on to their identity and belief system. They become incapable of seeing fault in themselves because it is always easier to blame the situation or the other person.

Resilience starts with an ability to see your weaknesses and the willingness to change in order to make yourself better. Examine your attitudes and the beliefs that make you who you are. Are you quick to generalize and make assumptions about people? Do you always have to win every argument to feel good about yourself? Do you know how to compromise? Can you say sorry when you are wrong? Are you still holding on to emotional baggage from your past relationships?

All these little things combine to influence how we see the world. They taint our experiences by making us only see what we want to see and overlook anything that goes against our beliefs. This is the kind of fixed mindset that makes people risk-averse. They are so used to thinking and acting in a certain way that doing something out of their norm is almost impossible.

If you are not willing to take risks and open yourself up to new ways of thinking and new experiences, it will only mean that your life will be restricted to a very small box. This box is the comfort zone that you have created for yourself. It is what you use to determine what you can and cannot do. This comfort zone is why you tell people, *I can't do that I am not good at it*, or *I am just a geek why would she go out with me*, or *I am such a slob, I will never get back into shape.*

Note that all these statements are assumptions that you have made about yourself and not facts. Yet by using them as a basis for your decisions you essentially keep reinforcing them with your actions. You believe you cannot do something so you do not bother trying or you believe someone is out of your league so you do not ask them out. In this way, you lose the battle on the inside before you can even try. That is how self-limiting your beliefs and attitudes can be. Overcoming self-sabotage starts with a willingness to shed beliefs and values that are no longer working for you.

Failure is only useful when you can use it as a lesson. Each time you fail, look for what you did wrong and what you did right. Carry the strengths forward and leave the weaknesses behind. Eventually, you will find that each time you fail you come out a little stronger because you identified something that stopped you from succeeding and you ditched it. If you cannot learn from failure and change who you think you are, you will always feel like you are banging your head against an invisible wall.

Stop Making Emotional Decisions

If you stop to examine all the times you have given up or quit, you can always trace it back to negative emotions. You were afraid to fail so you did not try, or you got angry when you were rejected so you gave up, or you felt miserable so you ended up binge eating and so on. Most of the emotional decisions that we make are driven by a need to make ourselves feel better in the moment.

When you make emotional decisions, you seek out instant gratification. You find it hard to persevere because you only want to experience the parts that feel good. This is the problem that many people face when trying to achieve a certain goal or stay on the right track. They simply cannot regulate their emotions.

Mental strength requires discipline because without discipline you will always be a prisoner to your emotions. It is discipline that will make you go to the gym even when you do not feel like it, or show up to work on time every day or study instead of going out partying. Discipline is the only real weapon you have against your emotions and this makes it the foundation of mental toughness.

But how do you use discipline to stop making emotional decisions? The easiest way to do this is to remove emotions from the equation. Create habits and schedules that set out a clear path for you to follow. For instance, if you know that each day you have to go to the gym in the morning, this will become a routine in a matter of days and before you know it becomes an automatic habit. This is more effective than just waiting to feel like going to the gym. By establishing a routine, you create a deliberate action and path to your goal without banking on emotions.

Most often emotions direct our decisions when we do not have a plan laid out. When you make a plan, the decision is already made beforehand so all you have to do is follow-through. There is no longer a question of if you will do it because it has been planned ahead of time. For example, if you plan to eat healthily, start by removing all the junk food from your fridge or pantry. This will mean that even if you feel the urge to binge eat you will not have access to any junk food so by default you will have to stick to the plan you have put in place.

Develop a routine that sets out a clear path to follow. With time you will realize that mental strength is like a muscle. The more you use it the stronger it becomes. Overcoming your emotional impulses will be hard at fast but once the routines you have set in place become entrenched habits you will find yourself doing the right thing almost automatically.

When you rely on motivation or willpower you will only do things when they feel good or when you feel like it. However, if you establish clear routines and schedules, then you will have a deliberate path to follow that leads you from where you are now to where you want to be. Make it a mission to not just have goals but to also have a plan and a deliberate course of action.

Chapter 5: Turnaround Toughness

Let's revisit Dave's situation for a minute. Dave has lost his job, his wife and he is on the verge of losing his house. So how does he deal with his situation? Is there a way back when at the prime of your life you find that everything you worked for is suddenly gone? When things fall apart and everything that could go wrong does go wrong, what do you do in such a situation?

Turnaround toughness refers to the kind of mental strength that enables you to recover from failure. This type of mental toughness is about resilience and the ability to reinvent yourself. When most people find themselves facing defeat after defeat, they sink lower and lower into nothingness until they can barely remember who they were or what they were aiming for. The despair makes them give up on their dreams and they resign themselves to just existing.

Consider a man who finishes colleges and cannot seem to land a job of any kind. He applies to thirty jobs and is rejected every time. He even applies for a job flipping burgers at KFC but that too does not work out. As if that is not enough, he is also rejected by Harvard ten times. When you think of so much rejection and failure it is almost impossible to imagine going on yet Jack Ma did not just go on but he founded a multibillion company.

The founder of Alibaba was rejected over thirty times before he went on to become the richest man in China. Without his resilience and turnaround toughness, Jack Ma would probably have slipped into oblivion like so many people do when they face failure after failure. Yet it is failure that seems to create more success stories than anything else. Failure builds perseverance it fuels determination and in some few people, it gives them even more reason to fight for their dreams.

When it comes to mental toughness, turnaround toughness is probably the most important aspect. This is because there is always the possibility of failure. No matter what you are pursuing, big or small, there is always a risk that things might not go your way. If you have turnaround toughness, you will be able to take any setbacks in stride and keep moving towards your goal. Like Jack Ma, you will find a way to get back up every time you fall because you have goals that are worth fighting for.

Resilience is not the easiest thing to build. Often when you have been discouraged, rejected, and told that you are not good enough, you want to simply give up and stop getting hurt. Because the truth is rejection hurts and nobody likes pain. However, if you can cultivate turnaround toughness you will be able to repurpose that pain and use it to re-energize your efforts. That ultimately is the power of turnaround toughness; being able to embrace failure and use it as a lesson to make yourself better.

Acceptance

One of the biggest pitfalls that can interfere with your mental strength is an inability to accept your situation. Denial makes it easier to deal with tough situations because it gives you a way out of your guilt and absolves you of the responsibility for your mistakes. When things really go wrong, the most important thing you can do is to first of all accept the failure.

Many people waste years of their life by refusing to accept the situation. They stay in dead-end jobs or they suffer in toxic relationships or in some cases they refuse to accept that they need to change. When you cannot accept the situation that you are in, you will be powerless to change it because essentially you are trying to hide behind half-truths or lies.

If for example, you lost your job because you did something wrong. There are two ways you can deal with it. One, you can accept responsibility for your mistake, make amends for what you did, and then move on to the next opportunity. On the other hand, you can adamantly refuse to accept that you were wrong and use all your energy trying to justify your actions or shift blame to other people. In one scenario you are giving yourself a clean slate from which to start again and in the latter, you are hiding from the truth.

Every time you find yourself at the end of your rope you have these two options. You can accept where you are and take responsibility for fixing it or you can find comfort in victimhood and stay where you are. Turnaround toughness requires that you develop the capacity to own your mistakes. Not so that you can punish yourself for them, but so that you can learn from them and move on.

Think of it this way, if you are always sweeping dirt under a rug, sooner or later the rug will not be big enough to cover the dirt. Denial may give you some relief from the hurt and the mental pressure but eventually, all your chickens will still come home to roost. Learn to be brutally honest with yourself and your situation. Acknowledge where you are and take responsibility for your own life. At the end of the day, no matter what the circumstances are or what the other person did, where you are in life is the sum total of the choices you have made. Nothing more, nothing less.

There is freedom in acceptance that allows you to start again and start with a clean slate. When you can look yourself in the mirror and say, *I screwed up, I need to change this situation*, then from this point on they will be nothing holding you back since you have gotten out of your own way. What people do not realize is that when you are in denial, you are the thing that is standing in the way of your progress.

Have enough courage to admit your mistakes, and acknowledge your situation. Only then can you effectively bounce back from failure and create new outcomes for yourself. Remember that a big part of resilience lies in your ability to reinvent yourself which you can only do if you willingly accept your faults and seek to fix them. If you have been walking around with self-limiting beliefs or attitudes that led you to fail in the first place, you can only bounce back by shedding those beliefs and attitudes that are no longer serving you.

Let us say you work in a competitive corporate environment. You have spent years and years in the same position with no signs of advancement. Now in this situation, you can put it down to bad luck, or maybe an unsupportive boss and explain the situation away. However, if you choose to look inward and see how you may have caused the situation you may discover that you probably have more to do with your career stalling than you realize.

To truly accept your circumstances, you must be willing to get uncomfortable by examining yourself, your beliefs, and your behavior. Have you conducted yourself in a way that inspires trust and confidence? Do you step up to take on tasks that other people stay away from? Are you conscientious in your work or do you just do enough to get by? When you ask yourself such questions you can unravel bad habits that may be costing you more than you think.

To truly bounce back from failure, acceptance is the first step. When you acknowledge the situation, it means that you are ready to process it and get over it.

Processing the Truth

If an addict goes to Alcoholics Anonymous or any other kind of rehabilitation program, they are encouraged to first acknowledge that they are addicts. This process is meant to help the person face reality and accept the truth of their situation. Many people who remain stuck in addictions are those that cannot process the truth of their situation. They will say things like, *I can quit anytime I want* or, *I don't have a problem I am only doing this because I am depressed* or similar excuses.

An addict has to be willing to admit their addiction before they can recover. Similarly, any time you are faced with failure your ability to bounce back will depend on whether or not you can process the truth of your situation. This means not looking for scapegoats, blaming it on the circumstances, or the competition. Mentally strong people focus on the things they can control and do not waste energy on things that are beyond their control.

If you spend time and energy lamenting the circumstances that you cannot control, you will remain trapped in failure because you are not in charge of your own life. Mentally tough people do what they can, where they are, and with what they have. They realize that often, life is not always going to go exactly the way you want it to so your power lies in what you can control.

To build your resilience and your ability to bounce back focus on the things we can control. For example, during the Covid-19 pandemic, businesses had two options. They could adapt to the situation and adjust the way they operate to survive in a difficult situation or they could sit and wait for the pandemic to end. In this scenario, you have no control over the circumstances but you still have control over how you react to it.

The businesses that were able to stay afloat during the lockdowns that followed the pandemic are the ones that pivoted to adapt to change. They found ways to reach their clients either through online platforms or offering home delivery services or any other measure that gave them a chance to continue operating. This is what it means to bounce back. You will not always be in control of the situation but you can control how you react to it.

Understand that failure is just an indication that something did not work. This means you have the opportunity to try a different approach or something else altogether until you get the result you want. Think of failure as a roadblock. It does not mean that the destination is no longer there; it simply means that you may need to find an alternative route to get to the destination. People who take failure as a final result always end missing potentially great opportunities because they let one setback diminish their hope.

Think of J.K Rowling who had to bounce back from twelve rejections in order to get Harry Potter published. She had 12 chances to simply give up and throw her manuscript in the trash but instead she kept going. This is what turnaround toughness is all about. It means that you can see past the failure and realize that just because one person or two do not like your idea or product it does not mean you have the wrong product. You simply haven't found the right audience for it.

Processing the truth is not telling yourself, *I am a failure*, or *I never get anything right*. It is acknowledging that something did not work out but you still have a chance to try again and until you get it right. When an athlete comes last in a race or second last. They do not give up their career. Instead, they go back to the training ground and keep trying. They understand that the more they train the better they will get at their sport.

To become tougher mentally you must process the truth in such a way that you can see the missteps you have made and use them as lessons to forge the way forward. By focusing on what you can control, it becomes possible to persevere through even the most challenging situations. Break down your goals into small milestones that you can walk on daily without feeling that you are facing an insurmountable mountain.

Half of the problem with challenges is how we frame them. Consider the common example of David and Goliath. David and his fellow Israelites were looking at the same enemy. However, the soldiers saw an enemy so big that he could not be beaten so they did not even bother trying. David on the other hand saw a target so big it would be impossible to miss. Sometimes by reframing the challenge you are facing, you can find a solution or a way through that you never thought possible.

To achieve turnaround toughness, you must be flexible enough to change your point of view, adjust your beliefs, and even seek help where necessary. Mental strength does not mean remaining obstinate or stubborn against a reality that does not conform to your values. Mentally strong people identify new perspectives and new belief systems that help them get back on their feet after a setback.

Learning from Failure

In difficult times it is hard to see any possible good that could come from failure. Yet the most valuable lessons we can learn are from the mistakes we have made. Learning from failure is an integral part of turnaround toughness because it means you will not repeat the mistakes that you have made in the past.

Resilient people know that every failure comes with an opportunity to learn no matter how painful the lesson is. A person who goes bankrupt on their first attempt at business is likely to be more careful the second time around. A student who flunks their exam is likely to change their study habits and so on. Failure gives you an opportunity to identify and overcome your weaknesses and bad habits.

The trouble with failure is that for people who are not mentally strong, failure leads to fault finding. This is what happens when every time something goes wrong in your life, you start looking for someone or something to blame. You failed your exam because the teacher does not like you, you missed the deadline because you were caught in traffic or the weather was horrible so you did not go for your morning jog. Whatever the case is, when you feel the need to explain away your failure by pointing at someone or something else, you miss a valuable opportunity to improve yourself.

Acceptance and facing the truth are the only way you can build up your resilience and ability to get back on your feet after failure. Mentally tough people do not waste energy trying to figure out who to blame. Instead, they focus on getting better and improving themselves. They admit their weaknesses and missteps and recognize the faults in their actions that contributed to the failure.

There are plenty of reasons why you may fail to achieve your goal. It could be that you failed to plan for what you needed to do and ended up getting blind sighted by unexpected circumstances. You may have lacked the necessary skills to undertake the task. It could be that the task that you had required more time than what you had or in some cases you could fail due to inattention or lack of focus. In any of these scenarios, if you accept your role in the outcome, you will recognize what you need to change. This is why acceptance is crucial when it comes to learning from failure.

It is better to admit defeat and start again than to be stuck in a rut permanently because you are unwilling or unable to admit your mistakes. As emotionally unpleasant as it may be, analyzing failures may help you develop resilience because it will help you understand your blind spots. We all know people who are perpetually jumping from one bad relationship to another. This becomes a repetitive cycle and they may even start to label themselves as "unlucky in love".

Luck, however, has little to do with it. Unless you can analyze objectively what went wrong in your past relationships what will stop you from making the same mistakes in the next one? If you have a tendency of experiencing the same failure over and over again, whether it is in your relationships, at work or financially, it only means that you are not learning from your mistakes.

The common cliché *shame on you if you feel me once, shame on me if you fool me twice* is a very apt assessment of what should happen when you fail. It simply alludes to the fact that if you fail the first time, it could be due to unavoidable circumstances but if you fail again, it simply means you did not learn your lesson.

Turnaround mental toughness is the ability to see your failure, analyze it, and draw valuable lessons from it.

Moving forward or bouncing back doesn't mean cruising past your mistake because you are afraid to dent your ego. True resilience stems from understanding where you went wrong, accepting it, and then moving on. People who refuse to learn from their mistakes are bound to repeat them. Do not fall into this trap. Failure will only be a precursor for success if you learn from it. Ignoring it, blaming others, finding comfort in victimhood, or simply refusing to acknowledge is a sign of lack of mental strength and a sure way to sabotage your progress.

Moving On

The most important part of turnaround toughness is of course actually moving on from whatever setback life throws your way. Essentially how well you can pick up the pieces and keep moving after failing will be determined by how mentally strong you are. For most people recovery from failure is so difficult that they end up giving up on their goals altogether because they feel like the wind has been knocked out of their sails.

To achieve the extraordinary, you must be willing to go to extraordinary lengths. You have to keep your passion and commitment to your goals no matter what the circumstances are. The one thing that sets mentally strong people apart from the rest is that they keep their discipline no matter how they feel, or what the external circumstances are. It is this discipline that will help you overcome self-pity, fear, and even disillusionment.

To move on one of the most important things you will have to do is cultivate self-discipline. Self-discipline is the capacity to control yourself. It enables you to commit to deliberate actions and behavior that will help you get what you want. Think of sportsmen training or navy seals going through their training. Of course, these people do not always feel like training but their discipline enables them to commit to a schedule and a mission regardless of what else is going on. This kind of dedication and commitment helps them to build habits that in turn create solid plans of action that enable them to reach their goals.

When you are at the bottom of the barrel and you want to give up, the best way to get out of this funk is by investing in plans, schedules, and deliberate actions. This is because a schedule or plan of action will help you get past the emotional turmoil. Imagine if every day you have a schedule of things that you need to do, when to do them, and for how long you need to do them. When you outline such clear plans, even when you are feeling under the weather you still know what you should be doing. This will give you the drive to get going and start moving.

When it comes to moving on, investing in a process or course of action is what people who are mentally tough do. Do not wait for inspiration or the right mood to strike. Identify your goal, then identify deliberate steps that will help you achieve your goal. If this means writing down a to-do list every day, do it until the actions you take every day start to become habits. For example, if you want to live within your means and save more money, you can plan to save a certain amount each month. Make sure that you deposit this amount every month before you budget for anything else. This will help you stick to your budget and avoid overspending.

No matter what your goals are, focus on small but deliberate actions that will move you closer to your goal. Avoid situations why you overwhelm yourself with long lists of things to do and instead stick to two or three effective habits that you can commit to consistently. Avoid quick-fix solutions that fall apart after a few days and instead look for sustainable, long-term daily steps that will help you stay on course.

Picture a person who goes to the gym each day for three hours for a week then quits and a person who exercises each day for 30 minutes. Of course, the one with the long-term plan may have slow results but they will be permanent. Do not be tempted to go for quick fixes or 180-degree turns. Instead, invest in long term habits that will result in real results in the long term.

It is natural to look for shortcuts after failure. This is because you are trying to make up for lost time or erase the effects of the failure as quickly as possible. However, if you try and overcompensate, you may end up right where you started or even worse off. Instead of trying to calm the storm, calm yourself is a good mantra to live by. What this means is that taking time to process what happened and then waiting until you are calm enough to try again is the best way to deal with tough situations.

When you make decisions in the heat of the moment, chances are that these decisions will be emotional. We all know that emotional decisions are not always the most logical. So before you quit your job because your boss shot down your pitch, or quit college because you flunked your exam, or whatever other situation you find yourself in, take some time to absorb the truth, process it, and then make a decision calmly. Mentally strong people are good at finding ways to de-stress. This is because they understand that making decisions under duress can lead to even bigger mistakes.

If you have just suffered a setback, could be a divorce, job loss, bankruptcy, or anything else, before you settle on what to do next, take some time to just process and deal with your loss. Trying to move on with a load of emotional baggage will cloud your judgment and cause you to make decisions from a place of anger or fear.

Yoga, meditation, confiding in someone you trust, and good old exercise are some simple but effective ways to deal with stress. You can also remove yourself from the situation for a while and put some distance between you and the problem. The most powerful weapon you have when trying to bounce back is a clear mind so find a way to de-stress before coming up with your next plan of action.

Finally, once you have put the anger, regret, or hurt behind you, the final step is to focus on your strengths. Most people get trapped in cycles of self-pity because when they fail all they see is the negative. Do not keep beating yourself up over what happened. Focus on the positives by thinking about other times when you did not fail or when you excelled.

Holding on to the positive will give you the confidence to try again. Do not let failure take away your self-esteem. Remember everybody fails, but those who are mentally tough get back up each time better and stronger than they were before.

Chapter 6: Critical Moment Toughness

Freezing or chocking at critical moments is something that a lot of people face when they are put on the spot. Whether its performers getting stage fright just before an event or someone suffering a panic attack before making a public speech or forgetting everything the minute you sit down for an exam. In critical moments it is natural to get overwhelmed and choke.

The problem with chocking at critical moments is that often you will easily forget things that you know. Your mind goes blank and you struggle to think coherently. This kind of reaction to pressure can cause you to mess up great opportunities because when the big moment comes you are unable to perform under pressure. Critical mental toughness is the mental strength that enables you to hold up well under pressure and remain calm in difficult situations.

Maybe you have been waiting for an opportunity to interview for your dream job all your life. However, when the moment finally comes and you are sitting across from an interview panel, you panic, and all the things you wanted to say become a jumble of words. Or, all you ever wanted was to be a lawyer, but when its finally time to take the bar exam, you freeze because under the pressure to perform you can barely recall anything that you studied. These kinds of choke or freeze moments happen to many people because they do not have critical moment toughness.

When you are under pressure, your body goes into flight or fight mode. Your body is naturally designed to react to fear or threats by activating the flight or fight response. This response is initiated by the nervous system and its main goal is to prime you to fight or run away from danger. This is why you will notice that when you are scared, or threatened, your heart rate quickens, your breathing becomes faster and you even start sweating more than usual. All these reactions are geared to making you physically more capable of either fighting off a threat or running away from it.

This flight or fight response is invaluable because you need it to stay safe from danger. If you are being pursued by a marauding bear or a rabid dog, you certainly want the extra reserves of energy to run for your life. However, your body's flight or fight system cannot differentiate between a physical threat and an emotional threat.

This means when you are freaking out about an interview or an exam or any other situation, your flight or fight system kicks in just as it would if you were running from a burning building. In essence, whether the threat is physical, emotional, or even imaginary, your body's response to stress is the same.

Unfortunately, when the fight or flight response is active in your body, your ability to think clearly is impaired. All the brain reserves are directed to dealing with the potential threat so your forebrain which is the rational brain is no longer in charge. This effect of stress on the brain is what makes people freeze in critical moments. Mental pressure, therefore, goes much deeper than simply being an emotional reaction to actually affecting mental clarity and as a result affecting your performance.

This means that your ability to stay calm under pressure is what can make the difference between underperforming or excelling in critical moments. Critical moment toughness is what enables some people to be comfortable in high-pressure situations and take things in stride without choking. Mentally strong people know how to cope with high-pressure situations because they are able to regulate their emotions.

Calmness Under Fire

In more ways than one, critical moment toughness has a lot to do with your emotional intelligence. Emotional intelligence is based on two main competencies. These are personal competencies and social competencies. The first aspect of emotional intelligence is personal competence.

Your level of personal competence is fundamentally based on your ability to understand and regulate your emotions. This means that to be personally competent you need to be first aware of your emotions, your emotional triggers, and how you react to these emotions. The second part of personal competence is the ability to regulate these emotions. In essence, your level of emotional intelligence will depend on your level of self-awareness and your ability to self-regulate or your self-discipline.

The other aspect of emotional intelligence is social competence. This refers to your ability to understand other people's emotions and respond appropriately to them. It also covers your ability to manage relationships. This second aspect of emotional intelligence determines how well you play with others or your people skills.

People with high levels of emotional intelligence have a higher level of critical moment toughness. This is because they can regulate their emotions better so they do not get overwhelmed by stress or pressure easily. In addition, they understand other people better so they are more competent in dealing with high-pressure situations where they have to interact with other people.

In essence, there is a direct link between your level of emotional intelligence and how well you are able to deal with high-pressure situations. This means that to develop critical moment toughness you need to cultivate emotional intelligence. We have already explored the role that self-discipline plays in your ability to achieve your goals. The significance of self-discipline is that it enables you to manage your emotions in such a way that your decisions are not based on emotional reactions or impulses.

To become more emotionally intelligent, you have to cultivate self-awareness. This means being aware not just of your emotional reactions but also of the triggers behind those emotions. For instance, if you always freak out when you need to speak in public or make a presentation, do you understand why you feel that way? Are you afraid of being judged? Is it because you are ill-prepared for the moment? Or are you intimidated by the other people in the room?

When you understand emotions as a reaction to an underlying belief or thought then you can begin to understand what causes your emotions and how to control them. Let's say for instance that you are afraid of sitting for an exam because you are afraid you will fail. In this case, your fear is not of the exam in itself but rather of your ability to pass the exam.

So if your fear is being caused by self-doubt then the only way to get past this fear is by addressing the self-doubt. This means if you can get to the root or the trigger of the emotion, you will be able to process your emotions in such a way that they do not influence your actions or behavior.

Self-awareness does not mean that you do not experience any emotions. Rather it is about understanding your emotions and what causes them. This understanding helps you to manage your emotions better and regulate your behavior. Some people for instance respond to stress by comfort eating. The only way they can kick this habit is by first understanding what triggers their emotional eating. Once they unravel the cause then they can look for healthier ways to deal with stress.

Without self-awareness, it is difficult to manage your emotions because you have no idea what is causing them. Maybe you get stressed out at interviews because the first interview you went to was a train wreck so you created a negative emotional association for interview situations. Or you flopped at a sales pitch once, so every time you need to make a presentation or pitch your mind immediately goes to negative emotions.

Emotional triggers are varied and some may even be irrational. However, it is important to have a keen understanding of your emotions so that you are able to control them effectively. Simple habits such as journaling, meditation, or breathing exercises can help you get in touch with your emotions and get better at processing your emotions. When you find a healthy outlet for your emotions, they stop clouding your judgment and affecting your ability to think clearly.

Ever heard of the old wives' tale that you should count to ten whenever you are feeling angry? This simple technique works in helping you to manage your emotions because it allows you to think rationally before acting out. When we encounter any situation or experience, our first reaction is on an emotional level. This is because any stimuli we encounter is first processed in the limbic system of the brain. This limbic system is where emotions are generated. Once these stimuli or experience has been interpreted emotionally in the limbic system, it is then passed on to the forebrain. The forebrain is where logical or rational thought takes place. This is the biological pathway that our bodies naturally take when interpreting experiences, situations, or thoughts.

What this means is that the emotional brain reacts faster than the rational brain. Essentially what counting to ten does is give time for your rational brain to catch up with the emotional brain. This is why taking time when you are feeling angry or overwhelmed can help to give you a better perspective of the situation at hand and how best to deal with it. To remain calm under fire, you must get into a habit of processing emotions first before reacting. This is the only way to cultivate critical moment toughness.

The social competence aspect of emotional intelligence is also fundamental when it comes to remaining calm under fire. This is because when you are aware of other people's emotions you can manage your interactions better. Think for example of the anxiety many people feel when they have to address a group of people, go for an interview or interact with other people. Most of this anxiety comes from not knowing what the other person is feeling or how they will respond to you.

When you have to interact with others, it is common to be anxious about whether or not you will be judged, whether you will be understood, and even whether or not the other person will like you. Social awareness equips you to understand and read other people's emotions so that you can understand them better. As a result, social awareness enables you to have better interactions. This is the skill that sets apart great negotiators from average negotiators.

A great negotiator can read the other person's mood. They know when to push, when to pull back, and when to close the deal. This kind of emotional intelligence is crucial when you want to attain critical moment toughness. You will notice that most of the situations that exert the most pressure on you, are situations where you have to perform in the presence of other people. When you need to prove a point, win people over or get people to cooperate on some issue. In these situations, the pressure can be overwhelming especially if you lack social awareness and relationship management skills.

This means that part of cultivating critical mental toughness is building up your social awareness and relationship management skills. In high-pressure situations, it is easy to get so caught up in your emotions that you forget to pay attention to the other person. This makes you miss important cues that would otherwise have guided you on the best way to proceed or approach the situation.

For example, if you are delivering a presentation, you cannot just plod along without paying attention to your audience. You have to read their moods, observe the points that seem to elicit positive reactions and those that cause negative reactions. In this way, you can ensure that you are striking the right cords and avoid being out of touch with your audience.

The beauty of being socially aware is that it can actually help you to get past some of your anxiety. By focusing on the other person, you take your focus away from your own emotions and your level of anxiety starts to dissipate. This is because sometimes most of the pressure we feel is because we are too much in our own heads, overthinking and overanalyzing the situation. If you can instead focus on what the other person is thinking or feeling, you will minimize your fears and anxiety.

In an interview scenario or even when making a presentation, instead of only focusing on what you are feeling, try to instead think about the other person. *What does the interviewer really want to know with that question,* or *what questions would the client need to be answered about this product,* or *if I were in their shoes, what information would be really important?* When you ask yourself these kinds of questions, then it is no longer all about what your feeling or your anxiety but about the other person's needs.

When you can read your audience and understand other people's emotions it stops being all about your needs or your fears. The more you focus on others the less overwhelming your emotions become and you can manage the pressure of the situation calmly. You will not dread every meeting, gathering, or social event because you will have learned to focus on other people instead of dwelling on your emotions. A simple way to do this is by learning to listen actively.

Most of the time when in conversation people tend to plan what they are going to stay next instead of actually paying attention to the other person. Train yourself to really listen, and watch for non-verbal cues that could point to how the other person is feeling. Your emotional intelligence is intricately tied to your ability to understand other people. Do not make every interaction about your thoughts and needs. Put yourself in the other person's shoes and try and understand them. The more socially aware you become the less fraught your interactions will be.

Ultimately remaining calm under fire depends a lot on your level of emotional intelligence. It comes down to being able to regulate your own emotions and understand the emotions of the other people around you. High-pressure situations are a direct result of your feelings about yourself, other people, or the circumstances you find yourself in. Naturally, if you can control these feelings then your battle is halfway won.

The Power of Positive Thinking

Critical moment toughness is your ability to handle high-pressure situations and perform well in critical moments. This ability will be largely be determined by the kind of thoughts and emotions that you have during such moments. Mentally strong people keep a positive mindset regardless of the situation because they understand the more positive they feel the more confident they will be.

If you have watched pre-game press conferences before any major boxing event, you will see that both the opponents are usually confident that they will win. Nobody goes into a boxing ring preparing to lose. They all go to the match thinking that they will get the best of their opponent and emerge victorious. This kind of attitude is crucial in cultivating critical moment toughness.

Before any big moment or opportunity, you have to quash any negative self-dialogue and self-limiting beliefs so that you can handle the pressure of the moment. When you focus on the positives, you are essentially keeping anxiety at bay by recognizing that you have what it takes to do what needs to be done. In contrast, someone who is always focused on thoughts of failure will always find themselves choking and underperforming in critical moments.

To win a battle on any level, you must first believe that you can. Mentally strong people will not give you a list of the reasons why they are not qualified for the job. They are aware of their weaknesses but they choose to focus on their strengths. If the first things that come to your mind when faced with an opportunity or challenge are the last ten things that you did wrong, then do not be surprised if you always fail under pressure.

Learn to silence your inner critic by deliberating shifting your mind away from negative thoughts. Negative self-dialogue like, *I am underqualified*, or *the competition is so much better than me* or, *I failed the last time* and similar negative thoughts only serve to undermine your mental strength. Pay attention to the kind of thoughts and beliefs that you allow to dominate your mind. If you are always undermining your own confidence, how can you hope to tackle challenges or deal with high-pressure situations?

Just because you failed in the past does not mean that you will fail now. Using past experiences to talk yourself into a panic is essentially self-sabotage and will gradually make you your own worst enemy. It is always easy to remember the things that you did wrong and forget the ones that you got right. Before taking on a challenge or big opportunity make a conscious effort to focus on your strengths. Picture yourself succeeding and use that image to put yourself in a positive frame of mind.

Thoughts become reality and if you are always thinking that you are a failure that reality will soon materialize. Learn to dissociate yourself from past failures and mistakes. Resilient people do not dwell on their past failures or assume that just because something did not work out in the past it will automatically fail. A good rule of thumb is to learn to live where your feet are. This simply means learning to live in the moment.

If you stop to think about it, you will realize that most of your anxiety stems either from thoughts of negative past experiences or fears about the future. Worrying about the past or the future only adds unnecessary pressure to the situation you are facing. Practice leaving in the moment and judging each situation on its own merits.

Critical moment toughness requires objectivity and positivity. Practice self-affirmation to boost your confidence and help you stay positive. Simple self-affirming mantras like *I am talented and capable, I am beautiful and confident, I have the power to do something great, I have what it takes to do this*, can help you overcome anxiety and pressure. Learn to build yourself up as opposed to tearing yourself down.

Remember we all have weaknesses and strengths but you have a choice on what to focus on. Just like you can easily get into a habit of negative thinking, you can also get into a habit of positive thinking. The more you learn to put a positive spin on situations, the less daunting they will become and the more confident you will feel in critical moments.

If you are honest with yourself, most of the times that you have quit or given up on something you did so because of your own thoughts. You convinced yourself that you could not do it, or it was too hard or that you were too tired. We talk ourselves out of our dreams and goals more often than other people talk us out of them. This is because internal pressure is always stronger and more damaging than any kind of pressure you will face from the outside.

People who are mentally tough go through the same pressures and challenges that other people do. However, since they have more self-belief and confidence in themselves they approach these challenges from an *I-can-do-it* point of view. In contrast, people who lack critically moment toughness approach high-pressure situations with an *Oh-my-God-how-will-i-do-this* point of view. In both these situations, both people are facing the same challenge but one is reducing the pressure of the situation while the other is dialing up the pressure.

External pressure will only become an issue if you let it get under your skin and undermine your confidence. Think of what the famous Spartans of Greece did when faced with an enemy. They did not focus on what the enemy had or how many soldiers they enemy had. Instead, the Spartans focused on their own strengths by improving their strategy, training harder, and getting prepared for battle. When you can effectively learn to focus on the controllable, you will find that you can deal with high-pressure situations better.

To win in any situation you must first believe that you can. This means that instead of talking yourself out of taking on challenges, you have to start talking yourself into taking them on. Be like the boxer who goes into the ring expecting to win regardless of who the competition is. Learn to develop a positive mindset that highlights the positives and helps you to see past the negatives.

If you have to make a sales pitch or negotiate a business deal, focus your thoughts on a positive outcome. Go into the meeting expecting to win and this will help to not only relieve some of the pressure on you but also boost your confidence. Think of it this way, the more positive you are, the more confident you are, and

76

the more confidence you have the better you will be at getting things done.

Resist the urge to go into an emotional tailspin whenever you are faced with a daunting task. You can do this by being aware of the kinds of thoughts that you are focusing on. If you feel the negative thoughts of defeat, or failure start to creep up on you, change the narrative by focusing on something positive. Remember we said that in any challenging situation, you have two options. You can feed your fear or you can feed your confidence.

When you feed your fear it means that you are choosing to focus on the negatives and as a result, you only amplify the anxiety and pressure you are under. The more stressed you feel, the less clearly you think and ultimately this affects how you perform. We all know people who are brilliant and well-spoken amongst friends but when they have to talk to strangers they become a pale shadow of themselves. This is caused by the effect anxiety has on mental clarity.

In contrast, mentally strong people feed their confidence. They do not dwell on negative thoughts but rather they make themselves feel positive and confident by focusing on what they are good at. They amplify their strengths and choose to reflect on past successes instead of past failures. A mentally strong person will fail just like everybody else but they do not let failure define who they are.

You will find people who call themselves failures because they failed at something, or they brand themselves stupid or weak based on a past mistake. This kind of self-limiting beliefs stem from an inability to dissociate from past failures. When you let what happened in the past define who you are, then essentially you create a self-defeating narrative in your head about what you can and cannot do. This is why it is always important to be aware of the kind of labels you put on yourself.

Instead of defining yourself by the times you lost, define yourself by the times you won. This is the difference between mentally tough people and those who are not. Mentally tough people can take failure as a single event and not make it a predictor or yardstick with which to judge the future. Unfortunately, people who are mentally weak remain tied to their mistakes in such a way that they are always expecting the worst and thinking negative thoughts.

Having a positive mindset is one of the most liberating things you can do for yourself. Whether it is your professional life, your relationships, or even your financial goals, expecting to succeed puts you on the right track. Positive expectations prompt you to lay down solid plans that will help you to achieve your goals and overcome your fear.

Being positive means finding ways to turn negative thoughts into positive ones. It means reframing situations in a way that allows you to see them from a positive perspective. Here are a few examples of how you can turn negative thoughts into positive thoughts.

Negative mindset vs **Positive mindset**

I have never done this before >> I can learn something new.

This is too hard >> I will try doing this from a different angle

I do not have enough time >> I will re-arrange my schedule to find time

I cannot change >> I will take a chance

What if I fail >> What if I win?

It did not work the first time >>I know what not to do this time

Staying in Your Lane

When it comes to critical moment toughness staying in your lane is a crucial skill to master. Often people put so much pressure on themselves by comparing themselves with others or focusing on their competition. If you are one of those people who constantly feel the need to beat someone else or outdo others you will often find yourself stressed and constantly feeling pressured.

While competition is healthy and even necessary sometimes. Getting so caught up on what other people are doing drains you of energy and time. Instead of constantly looking over your shoulder to compare or copy what other people are doing, focus on building your own skillset, and getting better. Staying in your own lane helps in cultivating critical moment toughness because it helps you to avoid unnecessary pressure from things that should not really matter in the first place.

There are many people who have stalled in their careers because they focus so much on office politics that they forget their job description. If you get into the habit of always trying to compare yourself with others, you will always be stressed and under pressure. When an athlete is running, they do not keep looking over their shoulder to see how close the opponent is. All their energy and focus is on their own race because that is the only way to win.

Having enough confidence and self-belief that you are not constantly threatened by others is one of the indicators of a mentally strong person. Look at it this way, you only have so many resources in terms of time, energy, and brainpower. Do you really want to waste them on what other people or doing or use them to reach your own goals? Do not be one of those people who always feels the need to dim other's peoples' light so that you can shine. Mentally tough people stand out on merit not because the competition is weaker.

When you make negative comparisons between you and other people, you put yourself under undue pressure which in turn affects your performance. Different people are strong in different areas. That's why an organization will hire people with complementary skills in order to create a strong team. When you start to overlook your strengths because you are trying to be like someone else, in essence, you are reducing your value by neglecting the thing that sets you apart.

Mentally tough people do not feel the need to conform or fit in. They are happy to shine in their own way and forge their own paths. This enables them to handle pressure remarkably well because the only expectations that they have to live up to are their own. Imagine that you have to give a presentation after two or three of your colleagues have given theirs. The more you listen to them, the more you will start to compare your speech with theirs.

You will start thinking about how your own presentation will pale in comparison, or maybe how you are not as charismatic or engaging as your colleague. By the time you get up on stage to give your presentation, you will have worked yourself into such a frenzy and may end up messing up a perfectly good presentation. This kind of scenario where you are always putting pressure on yourself by trying to keep up with the Joneses can become a big hindrance to performance and productivity.

When you fall into the comparison trap, you will start being afraid to seize opportunities. Instead of focusing on your abilities, you will be focused on how someone else is better or more qualified. Every big moment will feel like you need to beat someone else instead of just doing what you are supposed to do the best way possible.

Critical moment toughness requires that you keep your eye on the ball. Forget the competition or the circumstances and ask yourself, *why am I doing this?* When you have a clear goal in mind, then you will not get distracted by the competition. Your mind will be able to prioritize what you need to focus on over what is not important.

Do not respond to high-pressure situations by lashing out or trying to put other people down, Run your own race and you will find that the amount of pressure you feel in competitive environments is no longer as debilitating as it was before. Remember that everyone has their own goals that have nothing to do with you or your goals. The route to achieving your goal is not going to be exactly the same as someone else's so ultimately comparisons are counterintuitive.

One of the best ways to stay in your own lane is to invest in your own progress. If you are studying for an exam, do not worry about how long other people are studying for or which methods they are using. Study in a way that helps you to understand your material best and study for as long as you need to. If you adopt a mentality where you try and do things because other people are doing them, you will be doing a disservice to yourself.

Some people take longer to understand things, others take a shorter time and others understand things differently. Do not use a cookie-cutter approach where you think that just because something worked for your colleague or friend it will also work for you. Customize your experiences and situations to suit your uniques skills, strengths, and abilities. This way you will effectively manage any peer pressure and keep your focus on what matters.

When you free yourself from the need to compare, you will find that you no longer have undue pressure to do things a certain way. You will find it easier to work at your pace and develop yourself in a way that matters to you most. Some people are so busy comparing themselves with others that they end up chasing dreams and goals that really have no meaning for them. Your goals should be the only things driving you in a certain direction. Not the need to fit in, or the need to beat someone else at something.

Ultimately the amount of pressure you have to deal with will come down to your ability to separate the small stuff from the big stuff. If you cannot identify what the big picture is and what the distractions are, you will keep running around in circles and getting nowhere. Identify your goals, and make them the point on which you focus. There will always be people in the same field going for the same things you want, but they are simply distractions and not the main agenda.

Mentally tough people develop razor focus that enables them to stay on course no matter what. With this kind of focus, all the external pressure you put on yourself like, *what will people think of me*, or *what if someone else is better*, will fade into oblivion.

Make it your business to mind your own business and invest in actions and plans that center around how you can make yourself better each day.

It Starts with Self-Belief

At its core, mental pressure stems from fear. When you are afraid that you are not up to the task, you feel pressured. When you are afraid that you do not have sufficient time to get something done you feel pressured. When you are afraid that you will fail, you feel pressured. The mental pressure you feel at critical moments comes from fear, but where does this fear come from?

Your performance anxiety or fear of failure is caused by self-doubt. When you do not have confidence in your ability or your skills, you doubt your ability to take on whatever challenge is in front of you. This results in fear This fear will inturn create mental pressure and stress. This means that to improve your ability to cope in high-pressure situations you must first deal with the self-doubt that causes fear.

Self-belief is what causes people to take chances, step out of their comfort zones, and stay committed to their goals even in difficult situations. When you have confidence in your skills and abilities, you will not be deterred easily from pursuing your goals. This is because you already know that you can achieve your goals with time and effort. This kind of self-belief is what fuels passion, commitment, and dedication to goals.

People who believe in themselves do not give up on their dreams because they know that those dreams are within their reach. This kind of self-belief is what will make some people try thirty times when others give up after one set back. How much confidence do you have in your abilities? Are you aware of your strengths, your value, and what you have to offer?

Often, people want others to believe in them yet they do not believe in themselves. Any salesman will tell you that it is pretty difficult to sell a product you do not believe in. You have to first know your worth and your value before you can communicate it or express it to the world.

Self-belief is built on having a healthy self-esteem. It means trusting that you are capable of handling whatever is before you. When you believe in yourself you understand that nothing is impossible. This kind of confidence is crucial when dealing with high-pressure situations. It enables you to take chances, venture out of your comfort zone, and manage emotions such as fear.

People who are more confident are often preferred as candidates for positions over less-confident candidates. This is because people who believe in themselves are proactive and good at getting things done. They do not procrastinate because they are not afraid of failing. Instead, they readily take on challenges because they trust their abilities and judgment.

No matter how brilliant you are, if you do not believe in yourself, you will often feel under pressure because you do not have faith in your own abilities. Instead of approaching challenges as an opportunity to utilize your skills and acquire new ones, you will often feel anxious and apprehensive about doing something new. This is how a lack of self-belief can undermine even the most brilliant people.

To seize any opportunity, you must first have the courage to try. Without trying you will never really know how it would have turned out. This means that self-belief is a fundamental element of mental toughness. Without it, you will be prone to feeling powerless and helpless in the face of difficult circumstances. You only feel overwhelmed by circumstances when you doubt your ability to overcome them.

Being self-assured does not mean that you are cocky or arrogant. It just means that you have healthy self-esteem and that you are aware of your abilities, your strengths, and what you have to offer. Be vigilant about quashing self-limiting beliefs. These are beliefs that start with *I can't, I am not, I never, I shouldn't* and anything else that makes you feel incapable or ill-equipped. These thinking traps can turn ordinary situations into seemingly insurmountable challenges.

Be your own cheerleader by acknowledging and celebrating your strengths. Adopt a can-do attitude and make it your mission to always push yourself outside your comfort zone. Be self-aware and know what your strengths are and the weaknesses that you need to improve on. When you know who you are, you will not need others to validate or approve of you. You will be confident in your skills, abilities, and actions because you trust your own judgment.

Ultimately how well you handle pressure is determined by two key factors. How much self-belief you have and how well you can regulate your emotions. If you cultivate these two traits in yourself, you will find that you no longer freeze or choke in critical moments. You will have less stress to deal with in your life and ultimately you will have no problem committing to your goals and achieving them.

Chapter 7: Endurance Toughness

Fatigue does not just occur on a physical level. Fatigue can be emotional or mental. Physical fatigue takes a toll on our bodies but it is the mental exhaustion and emotional fatigue that can make the achievement of your goals almost impossible. When you feel emotionally drained and mentally fatigued, it becomes really difficult to keep going, and often, you will just give up because you no longer have the mental strength to keep going.

Mental fatigue occurs when you have tried repeatedly to come up with a solution to a challenging situation but you simply cannot seem to find one. When you are fatigued mentally, you see no way out of your situation so you end up quitting. Mental fatigue makes it difficult to see things clearly which of course makes it even more difficult to find a way out of your predicament. Most times when you give up on your dreams or goals it is because you are mentally fatigued and simply cannot muster up the mental toughness to keep going.

Emotional fatigue usually occurs when a situation has drained you so much emotionally that you simply want out. This is when you have been hurt or disappointed so many times that you simply cannot take the pain anymore. People who have gone through a series of bad relationships often end up suffering from emotional fatigue and giving up on love altogether.

Emotional fatigue can be really debilitating because it influences your actions and your habits. Bad habits like addictions can become an escape route for people who are seeking solace from emotional fatigue. It is not uncommon to be physically, emotionally, and mentally drained all at the same time. This kind of fatigue leaves you feeling empty and without the will to keep moving forward.

Endurance toughness is the kind of mental strength that enables you to overcome mental exhaustion and stay committed to your goal no matter what the circumstances are. Whether you are dealing with physical fatigue, mental exhaustion, or emotional fatigue, endurance is what will keep you moving forward. Endurance toughness enables you to keep your faith and hold on to your goals even through difficult circumstances. It means keeping your dedication and commitment no matter how you feel.

Endurance toughness is the most difficult type of mental toughness because it requires you to keep pushing yourself even when the easiest thing to do would be to simply give up. This kind of toughness is what will help you to keep pushing on when you are running on empty and cannot see a light at the end of the tunnel.

Just like physical endurance, mental and emotional endurance require that you go beyond the limits of what you think you are capable of. When people undergo physical endurance training, they usually train themselves to push past their physical limitations and increase their levels of stamina and physical strength. This is the same principle that applies to endurance toughness. It is the type of mental strength that teaches you to persevere through extenuating circumstances until you get what you want.

In endurance toughness, surrender is not an option. When you cultivate this type of mindset, you only have one option which is to see your mission through to the end. This means that you keep going on the days when you have zero motivation. It means that you keep going when you are stressed and anxious. It means that you keep going when you are physically and mentally exhausted. Endurance helps you to maintain your performance levels regardless of what circumstances are. This is the kind of mental toughness that we see in Navy seals.

Perseverance; The Science of Not Giving Up

Success is built on consistency and persistence. It does not matter how good your plan is if you are not able to follow through on it consistently until you get what you want. Unfortunately, most people fail to reach their goals because they are not consistent when it comes to pursuing them. People will follow the plans they have laid out until things get difficult or they get distracted. When this happens, they quit and give up on their goals altogether.

Endurance toughness is essential in achieving goals because it enables you to remain consistent even when things are not going your way. Even when you have the best intentions but you do not have the persistence or perseverance to follow through on your plans, you will not achieve what you set out to do. Let's consider, for example, Jill who is trying to lose weight.

Jill is overweight and her doctor has told her to lose at least forty pounds if she wants to remain healthy. This news makes her worry about her health and she resolves to do something about her weight. On the first day, she wakes up early and goes for a jog in the morning. She also makes a conscious effort to eat healthier and avoids junk food and unhealthy snacks.

As the week goes on Jill starts to feel sore and miserable. Her knees are aching, her stomach is always rumbling and she misses her favorite ice cream. By the fifth day, Jill has given up on jogging altogether and she is back to her regular unhealthy diet and habits. She tells herself she will get back on the weight loss program next week. This of course turns out to be an empty promise and her attempt at healthy living comes to an abrupt albeit predictable end.

Jill's case is not extraordinary. In fact, for most people, starting something and giving up on it when it gets hard is kind of a way of life. There are people who make a habit of quitting relationships, others quit jobs and others just cannot commit to any particular goal. This habit of giving up is one of the reasons why people end up living in a rut where they are not making any progress in their lives.

Perseverance is hard to cultivate because it requires you to stay committed to your goals no matter what the circumstances are. It is easy to stay on track when things are going smoothly. The real test of mental toughness happens when you find yourself facing unexpected setbacks and difficult situations. If you can persevere through adversity then your grit or endurance toughness will help you to reach your goals no matter what the situation is.

Even when it comes to something as simple as doing ten reps instead of five in the gym, this has more to do with your mental endurance than physical strength. This is because often you will get exhausted mentally long before physical exhaustion sets in. This means that to attain endurance toughness the real obstacle will be the kind of thoughts you focus on and your emotions.

How do navy seals manage to go through the rigorous training that is part of their program? They manage the grueling drills and taxing schedules because they commit to schedules and habits which effectively take emotion out of the decision. They simply get up and do what they need to do without stopping to think about it. In developing endurance toughness and the ability to persevere, there is very little room for emotion or motivation. Perseverance is built on consistency, dedication, and self-discipline. It is these traits that enable you to overcome the emotional impulse to quit.

When you go by emotions, your natural instinct is to do things that feel good. Emotions drive you to comfort and security. When you feel threatened or afraid your emotions will tell you to stop and retreat to a safe place where you no longer need to feel scared. When you are exhausted and in pain, emotions will tell you to stop so that your body can feel good. In all the cases where you have quit, the reasons that drove you to give up were emotional.

When you leave your goals up to motivation or inspiration you leave yourself open to failure because motivation is an emotion. Just like any other feeling, motivation will come in waves. One day you will be feeling on top of the world and raring to go, and the next you will be feeling disillusioned and discouraged. This is the pitfall that many people fall into. They wait until things feel right or for inspiration to strike before they can get moving on their goals.

When the motivation fades so will your efforts to pursue your goals. Real perseverance and endurance are built on habits and deliberate actions. It involves creating a plan of action with deliberate steps that you will follow each day regardless of what you are feeling. In essence, to achieve endurance toughness you must have enough self-discipline to manage your emotional impulses.

In navy seal training, you do not go to go out for drills when you feel like it or when the weather is nice and warm. Navy seals stick to their schedule regardless of their circumstances. Come rain or shine, they have to go through their drills every day. With this kind of discipline, they are able to cultivate a level of endurance that enables them to persevere through whatever conditions they will encounter in battle.

If you have a habit of quitting and leaving things undone because they have become too hard or inconvenient, the only way to beat this habit is by committing to schedules and deliberate action plans that give you a clear path to follow. This involves creating detailed to-do lists of things you need to each day without fail. Come up with weekly plans that move you closer to your goal and create schedules that require you to take deliberate actions each day to reach your goals. This will instill self-discipline and help you to avoid getting into the habit of quitting whenever things get tough.

Perseverance is about investing in the process. It is not enough to know what you want; you also need to know what you need to do to get it. When you have invested in the process then no matter how hard the going gets you will be able to stay committed because you know what you have to do, why you need to do it, and when it needs to be done. Every goal needs a plan and it is this plan that will help you to stay on track and fully committed to what you want to achieve.

If you focus too much on the result you want and neglect to invest yourself mentally into the process then you risk running out of steam halfway along the way.

People with extraordinary grit and endurance, feel disappointment and discouraged just like everybody else. However, since they have cultivated self-discipline and invested in schedules and habits, they are able to overcome these negative emotions and stay focused on their goal. Prioritize plans over moods, motivation, or emotional impulses. The more you do this the easier it will be to move past failure and disappointment and keep going.

To build perseverance you need to understand what is at stake or what you stand to lose by giving up on your goals. If you quit now, think of all the wasted time and effort that you have invested. Mentally strong people consider what is at stake and this helps to strengthen their resolve despite the circumstances and difficulties that come their way. Endurance is not deterred by difficulty but rather strengthened by it.

One of the things that people who have endurance toughness do in order to stay focused on their goal is to keep their minds on the things they can control. Often you will feel helpless when things that are beyond your control occur. We all know that sometimes things will happen that you have no control over. In such circumstances, the only thing that will help you to get past that hurdle is focusing on the things that you can control. This means instead of letting circumstances overwhelm you, you prioritize the actions that you can keep doing to get you close to your goal.

For people in business things like economic downturns, stock market fluctuations, policy changes, and new technology are some unexpected circumstances that you may not be able to control. In such cases, you can either give up and close up shop or you can find a way to pivot your business to adapt to the changes. This is what it means to focus on what you can control. In essence, to endure, sometimes you may not be able to change the situation but you can always change yourself.

Endurance toughness requires adaptability and a willingness to change. Just like you cannot get different results doing the same thing over and over, in some cases to keep going forward you may have to ditch bad habits, prejudices, and biases that are holding you back. Sometimes the difficult circumstances that you find yourself in will be a creation of your habits, attitudes, and beliefs. That is why it is always important to analyze your failures honestly so that you can learn from them.

Do not keep banging your head against a solid wall by refusing to change your perspective and beliefs. Sometimes an attitude adjustment is all you need to see situations in a different light. You cannot hold on to an identity or an idea that you have created in your mind of who you are or who you are not at the expense of your dreams. Endurance toughness requires boldness and a willingness to examine and question your beliefs. This flexibility and adaptability will make it easier for you to see beyond challenges and keep it moving.

To keep persevering through difficulty it is important to not allow yourself to get so caught up in the results that you miss the progress you are making along the way. take time to celebrate the small victories that you make along the way. This will help you stay positive and committed to your goal. For example, if you want to lose 20 pounds, do not forget to acknowledge the 2 or 3-pound losses that you make each week. One of the reasons people give up is because they are so caught up in the final result that they are unable to appreciate the small milestones they achieve.

Take time to breathe and just allow yourself to enjoy the flowers on your journey. Life is as much about the process of getting to your destination as it is about the destination itself. In between where you are and where you are going is where your life actually unfolds. Keeping your joy, learning to laugh at yourself, and doing things that you love each day will make the pursuit of your goals feel less like a struggle. When you are happy and positive it is easier to stay on track and committed to what you want to achieve.

Be Where Your Feet Are

If we revisit Dave's story at the beginning of the book, he is in a position that many people find themselves in. This is where you have invested so much of your blood, sweat, and tears into something and then it still falls apart. Dave in his case is wondering how in the world he can start all over again at the age of forty-two. He is thinking of how far he has come only to lose everything all at once.

One of the quickest ways to lose steam and give up on your goals is if you let your failures define you. Often you will hear people say things like *I am a middle-aged cliché* or *I am too old to try* or *I am going to be a spinster all my life*. When you make this kind of declarations you are basing your future on your past experiences and mistakes. These experiences or mistakes become self-limiting beliefs that make you feel like there is no point in even trying.

People with endurance toughness keep their determination by living in the present. They do not dwell on their failures or mistakes. They simply keep their eyes on their goals and let the past remain in the past. This is what it means to be where your feet are. It means existing in the present moment. When you get caught up worrying about the past, you can easily become discouraged and give up on ever realizing your dreams.

No matter what age you are, or where you are in life it is never too late to start over and push for your goals. Do not think that you are too far gone to achieve anything worthwhile. As long as you have goals and objectives that you are working towards, your life will always be meaningful. Just like you would not walk around all day every day carrying a backpack full of baggage, do not carry all your emotional baggage from the past into the future. Life is best for those who travel light.

Process your emotions as they happen and work through them so that you do not carry them into your future. Take up practices like yoga and meditation that help in boosting mindfulness and becoming more present in your life. If you keep looking back at where you are coming from, you will only slow yourself down by carrying forward self-limiting beliefs and emotions. Leave the past in the past and focus on what is going on in the moment where you are now.

When you feel your thoughts going back to the past, practice deep breathing to bring yourself back to the present. A simple way to do this is to close your eyes and breathe in deeply to a count of six. As you breathe in shut out any external stimuli or intrusive thoughts and simply focus on the sensation of the air entering your body. After the inhale, exhale deeply to a count of six. During the exhale just focus on the sensation of the air leaving your body. You can repeat this process for as long as you need to until you feel calm and in control of your thoughts. In this way, you can bring your thoughts back to the present.

Mindfulness helps you to stay centered and grounded in reality. Meditation and yoga are also great ways to de-stress and stay centered. Remember that to overcome mental fatigue and emotional exhaustion you need to find a way to release negative emotions. When you release pent up emotions, you can think more clearly and find the strength that you need to keep pursuing your goals no matter how challenging or difficult things get.

Being present is not just about releasing the hold that your past has over you. It also means that you do not waste time and energy worrying about the future. Worry is something that people get into the habit of doing without really realizing the toll it has on their mental strength and ability to persevere. When you are constantly worrying about what will happen tomorrow you gradually make stress a constant fixture in your life.

Worry takes your focus away from what you should be doing and makes you think of all the things that may or could go wrong. When worry becomes a way of life, every day you have to fight your despair to find the motivation to keep going. When you are reaching for a certain goal do not obsess over it or how far you are from achieving it. Instead, choose to focus on your plans and the things that you can do in the present. If you get the process right, then the results will take care of themselves.

People who have endurance toughness have mastered the art of living step by step, one day at a time. They understand that what is most important is what you are doing now to make it possible to reach your goals. The only things that you have power over are your actions in the moment. You cannot go back and change the past so dwelling on it serves no purpose other than to make you feel discouraged.

In the same way, what your future looks like will be determined by your actions today. This means that your focus should not be about worrying about what may or may not happen, but rather on what you can do today to make it possible to reach your goals tomorrow, This kind of mindset will help you stay on track because you will have broken down your goals into steps and milestones that you can stay focused on no matter what.

Try to keep your mental experiences to a minimum. Mental experiences are the thoughts and emotions that we have that have nothing to do with our present circumstances. These mental experiences occur when we get caught up in the past. Essentially mental experiences can affect how you feel and undermine your ability to persevere even when they have absolutely nothing to do with the task at hand.

Train yourself to focus and concentrate. This might mean working in an environment that is free of distractions. Get rid of painful reminders of the past such as mementos. For some people sharing their past with a friend or a therapist may help them to leave the past in the past. Find a method that works for you and free yourself from the burden of being constantly dragged down by your past.

To develop endurance toughness, learn to focus on the next step. Do not overwhelm yourself with what you need to do next week or next month. Concentrate on what you need to do today and in this way your goal will not seem so far out of reach. For example, if you want to lose weight, do not worry about what you will do tomorrow. Start by eating right today and when you get to tomorrow you can figure out the next step. If you want to go back to college for the degree you always wanted, start by applying to the college you want to attend then take it from there. Once you break down your goals into a series of steps, following through becomes just a matter of course.

With discipline and consistency, you will build endurance naturally without really needing to think about it. Consistent actions will evolve into habits and before you know it, working towards your goals will become a way of life and not just a chore you need to get through. As long as your mind is on what you need to be doing now you will find it easy to manage the setbacks that come your way.

Think of it as living day by day without really getting too caught up in yesterday's mistakes or tomorrow's worries. Your confidence in facing the future will come from knowing that you did the right thing today and that come tomorrow you will do the right thing again. This is one of the best ways to beat the emotional urge to give up or surrender; taking your goal one day at a time, one deliberate step after another.

The great thing about endurance toughness is that it will help you get past any kind of exhaustion. Whether it is physical exhaustion that is wearing you down, mental exhaustion, or even emotional fatigue, endurance toughness enables you to get past it and keep moving.

Trust Your Journey

Endurance toughness is built on patience and the ability to keep your passion through thick and thin. Wouldn't it be rather unfortunate if you ran a marathon only to give up a few meters before you get to the finish line? Yet this is what we do often with our goals and dreams. You work your ass off to get somewhere and when you are so close to getting it something goes wrong and you give up.

It may be cliché, but most of the worthwhile things in life are not going to come easy. What this means that it takes extraordinary endurance to achieve extraordinary results. Shortcuts and quick fixes may seem like an easy way out but real lasting results only come through following through on your plans and doing the hard work required to achieve your goals.

The reason why it so easy to give up and why so many people lack endurance toughness is that society has taught us to prioritize comfort and convenience over effort. Each day there are new technologies and advances that are designed to make our lives easier and more convenient. It is therefore no wonder that most people surrender at the first sign of a challenge or roadblock in their way. They are so used to seeking comfort and convenience that anything that requires effort is to difficult to do.

If you give in to the need for comfort and security, you will never really cultivate endurance and perseverance. Your goals should inspire you to do whatever it takes to achieve them no matter how hard the process may be at times. Avoid letting circumstances or other people deter you from pursuing your goals. Expect and anticipate opposition and strife. It is irrational to expect that everything will somehow just magically align to help you reach your goals. Failure is a necessary and sometimes an inevitable part of success.

People who are patient tend to have more endurance toughness than people who chase instant gratification. People who cannot prioritize their goals over pleasure will always have a hard time staying dedicated to their goals when things get tough. Get into the habit of looking at situations with a long-term view. Consider what your actions today will mean for you, two months, one year, and even five years down the road. This will help you understand which actions are important and which ones will only derail you from your goals.

Henry Ford, the founder of Ford filed for bankruptcy a total of five times before he could finally get his company off the ground. Yet he never stopped pursuing his dream or fighting to achieve his goals. It is not the people with the best business plans or the most brilliant ideas that actually make it but rather the ones who have the grit and extraordinary endurance required to go the whole nine yards.

For some people, a minor slip on their road like having an altercation with their boss, fighting with their spouse, or flunking an exam is enough to make them want to give up on their dreams. Having patience and understanding that it takes effort, time, and dedication to get to where you need to go is what will help you deal with both the big roadblocks and the minor setbacks that are bound to be on the path to your dreams.

To get what you want, you must be willing to sacrifice some comfort and commit to a process even when you do not feel like it. To do this you need to understand that the only way to reach your destination is by trusting the journey you must go through to get there. Expecting to see results overnight is only going to make you feel discouraged and push you to quit.

Endurance toughness helps you to realize that whatever is waiting for you at the end of your journey is worth the cost or effort you need to make today. People who stay discipline no matter how they feel are not any different from anyone else. They also enjoy comfort and security. However, what makes them persevere is the understanding that what is at stake is more important than instant gratification or temporary comfort. This is why it is crucial to set meaningful goals that you are passionate about.

Your goals should be meaningful and important to you. If you set goals just for the sake of it or just to please someone else, you will never be able to persevere through difficulty to reach them. People stay committed and dedicated to their goals because they have set goals that inspire passion and discipline for them. If being a lawyer or a doctor is all you have ever wanted, you will have no problem being dedicated to your studies. On the other hand, if you are only doing it to please your parents you will constantly have to fight boredom, emotional resistance, and lack of passion.

Trusting your journey also means being comfortable with failure if that is what it will take to get what you want. You cannot expect things to go right on the first try. The valuable lessons that you need to become better are in the failures that you will experience when pursuing your goals. After having to file for bankruptcy five times, you can be sure that by the fifth time, Henry Ford got really wise about finances because he had already made all the mistakes there were to make.

Do not let failure deter you or undermine your confidence. Failing is only an issue if you cannot muster up the strength to bounce back and keep going. People who have endurance toughness manage to keep a positive mindset even through the most difficult circumstances. They take failure as part of the process and understand that it is only a permanent result if you let it stop you.

When you hear about people like J.K Rowling, Richard Branson, or Thomas Edison, you will rarely hear about the times they failed because what they were able to achieve through perseverance eclipsed any failure, they may have hard in their journeys. All the things that are giving you sleepless nights today, will be nothing but blips on your radar when you look back on your journey after you achieve your goals.

To get some perspective, always look back at the things you have overcome in your past that seemed so difficult or daunting when you encountered them. This should give you the confidence to handle whatever life throws your way. When you consider what you have had to overcome to get where you are, the path ahead no longer looks so daunting.

Cultivate your endurance toughness by realizing that so far you have already survived all the worst days of your life. So, what is so big that you cannot work through it to realize your dreams? All of our journeys are unique and ultimately it is up to you to decide whether what is waiting for you at the end of the journey is worth persevering for.

Chapter 8. Risk Management Toughness

Every opportunity comes with an equal chance of failure or success. This means that to seize opportunities and take chances you must be willing to take a risk. People who have risk management toughness are not afraid of failure, they are more afraid of the opportunities they will miss by not taking any risk.

To cultivate risk management toughness, you need to be comfortable with uncertainty and challenging yourself. Often, we make decisions based on what best aligns with our beliefs and values. For instance, if you believe that you are better at one thing over another you tend to always go for opportunities that align with what you think you are good at. While this approach may be safe, you never really learn anything new by always doing the things you have always done.

People with risk management toughness are the ones who are not afraid to disrupt themselves and do something different. They challenge their beliefs and do not hesitate to go against established norms or accepted practices if that is what it takes to reach their goals. This kind of mental toughness that gives people the mental strength and willingness to take risks and reinvent the wheel is what led to the startup revolution.

Founders of mega-companies like Uber, Airbnb, and similar startups took extraordinary risks to get where they are today. In the natural sense, the biggest taxi company in the world should have taxis yet uber does not own any taxis. The founders of Uber found a way to disrupt the system and go against what is common and expected. It is only by taking a risk that other people would have labeled crazy or impossible that such startups are able to change the definition of what is normal and what is not.

This same concept of disruption and taking a risk by venturing into the unknown is what has made Airbnb such a huge success. These companies did not just go along with the accepted business practice but rather, they found a way to revolutionalize their respective industries and create a new normal. The thing about risks is that the size of the risk is almost always equal to the potential payoff. It, therefore, takes extraordinary mental toughness to be able to take on such huge risks when you cannot be sure of the outcome.

While you may not be looking to found the next mega startup, it is important to borrow lessons from these startup founders who took big risks to achieve extraordinary success. The truth is, no one gets to such heights by playing it safe. You must be willing to take chances even when they feel unsafe or threaten your sense of security. This requires mental strength and a willingness to embrace uncertainty.

For most people fear is the main driving force behind their actions. Every decision they make is based on choosing the option that carries the lowest risk. When you become risk-averse, you are always going to be limited to what you know and what feels safe. This is why risk management toughness is crucial for people who want to achieve extraordinary outcomes in their lives.

Risks do not always have to be huge to pay off. Sometimes simply doing something you would not normally do can get you past a hurdle that you have been dealing with for a long time. To see different results, you must be willing to do something different. That is a simple fact of life. Avoid getting into thinking traps where you have closed yourself into a safe box that defines what you can and cannot do. Test your limits, your beliefs, and your abilities by trying something new and opening up your mind to new perspectives.

Ultimately the biggest hindrance that people have to achieving their goals is the need to stay within a certain comfort zone. This desire to avoid uncertainty at all costs is what makes people become risk-averse and resistant to change. Think of people who are stuck in dead-end careers because they are too afraid to rock the boat. They know that they can do better but they remain stuck in limbo because they do not want to risk failure. This is a classic example of how adopting a risk-averse mindset can cripple you and prevent you from making progress in your life.

Overcoming the Fear of Failure

When you think of all the reasons why you hesitate to seize an opportunity or take a chance at something, you are likely to find that your hesitation is fueled by some sort of fear. Fear comes in many forms. Sometimes you may find other excuses to explain why you are not doing what you need to be doing yet all these excuses are just covering up fear.

You may say you do not have enough qualifications, or you are not ready for the challenge or that you do not have enough capital to start and so on. The bottom line is, no matter what excuse you use, it all comes down to the fear of failure.

When you get into a habit of being driven by your fears, any challenge that comes your way and threatens your security is quickly classified as a threat. Once you identify it a threat then you do anything in your power to avoid it or get away from it. this is why some people will never step up at work when there is an opportunity or take a chance by doing something they have never done.

In fact, there are plenty of people who have brilliant ideas that they will never execute. Ultimately when your fear of failure is much bigger than your passion or commitment to your goals, you will never muster up enough courage to go after what you want.

Think of someone who has been planning to start a business for years. They even have the business plan all drawn up and have identified the product they want to offer. However, at the thought of leaving a cushy job that offers job security and a source of regular income, they balk at the risk involved in starting a business from scratch. Ultimately their brilliant ideas remain just that. They spend their time dreaming about the future they wish they had but could never have the courage to pursue.

When you make fear the driving force behind the choices you make, do not be surprised if you end up living an average existence doing average things. A lot of people confuse being risk-averse with being careful. Taking risks does not necessarily mean that you are being reckless. People with risk management toughness are able to weigh their opportunities against what they stand to gain or lose by taking a risk.

For instance, if you are thinking of quitting your job to start a business. You do not just wake up one day and quit your job. A measured risk means that you have done due diligence, come up with a plan of action, and then made a decision fully aware of what you are taking on. Just like you, people who take risks have concerns about safety and security. However, they are also passionate enough about their dreams to take calculated risks if it means they have a shot at achieving their goals.

If you find yourself constantly choosing the safest option, you may be denying yourself the chance to seize potentially life-changing opportunities. As much as you want to seek security and comfort, you should understand that there is a price you pay for safety. This price more often than not is passing up on opportunities that would have given you the opportunity to realize your dreams.

The reason why the fear of failure is such a powerful de-motivator is because when we fail, we have to confront our shortcomings. Nobody wants to fail or feel like they do not have what it takes to succeed. A lot of our emotions and confidence are invested in who we think we are. So when you are forced to confront your flaws then you end up feeling like in some way you have lost your identity. this is why most people will shy away from doing something new because they are more comfortable doing what they already know.

Failure is only a deterrent for going after your goals when you let it become stronger than your passion. People who have risk management toughness find a way to manage their fear of failure in such a way that it does not stop them from chasing their dreams. They feel the fear but do not let it overcome their determination to succeed and pursue their goals.

Like every other emotion, your fear of failure is tied to an underlying trigger. These could be anything from childhood events that made you feel insecure or unsafe, or past experiences that ended up in failure, or just an inability to stretch your boundaries. Whatever it is that is the root of your fear, unless you confront it you cannot develop risk management toughness.

Most of our fears stem from unresolved underlying issues that have preconditioned us to think in a particular way. For example, you may be carrying around a belief that you do not have leadership skills because you did not do well in leadership roles at school. The problem with these kinds of assumptions and generalizations of your abilities is that they are all based on who you were in the past.

The fact is that we all grow and evolve with time and experience. So if you remain adamant in judging your abilities based on past mistakes, you are essentially stripping any lessons that you learned from your past failures. Stop attaching labels to yourself and learn to view yourself objectively. Do not think of yourself as "the guy who botched the presentation last month". Just think of yourself as a the guy who has an opportunity to do something great. Ditch the labels and the self-limiting beliefs and gradually taking risks will not be so daunting.

To overcome your fear of failure, learn to dissociate reality from the assumptions that you have made based on the past. Even if you have made mistakes in the past, it does not mean that you cannot learn and do better given the chance to try again. Mentally strong people do not seek comfort in an identity that is based on the past. They are comfortable trying new things and challenging their beliefs because they understand that it is the only way to grow.

When a child is learning to walk, they must first get up. They will fall many times before they finally get their balance right, yet the falling does not stop them from trying until they finally master the ability to walk. If a small child has enough courage to get back up when they trip, what is stopping you from trying something new? This same analogy applies to most new things that you will try in your life. In most cases, you will fail the first few times you try, but what you will learn in the process will be worth the effort.

Every time you choose to pass on an opportunity because it feels like too much of a risk, consider what you will be missing out on. If your dream if to start a business but you are too afraid to make a move, think of the freedom and independence that you are missing out on. Consider all the opportunities that you are missing out on by not taking the leap and following your dream. When you focus on what you stand to gain by taking the risk, then the fear will still be there but it will pale in comparison to what is at stake.

Think of all the things that you procrastinate about as a result of the fear of failure. Consider the many ways in which your self-sabotage by giving in to fear. You remain stuck in unhappy situations that you are fully capable of changing because the though that you are risking failure by trying leaves you unable to take the necessary steps.

In the larger scheme of things, the choice that you have to make is between going after your goals by taking a risk or giving up on your goals to avoid the risk of failure. This is essentially a choice between unhappiness and uncertainty. You can never be truly happy unless you pursue your goals and yet the uncertainty of the unknown prevents you from taking a chance. So, ultimately you have to choose whether you want to be unhappy in your comfort zone or chasing fulfillment by embracing uncertainty.

One of the biggest reasons why people experience a fear of failure is because of negative thinking. If you are always thinking of the worst-case scenario, then inevitably every challenge or opportunity will seem like it is bound to fail. Train yourself to have hope and positive expectations. Negative thoughts can keep you from seeing things objectively and cloud your judgment. Always weigh the possibility of failure against the possibility of success. Instead of thinking *what if I fail?* turn that around to *what if I win?*

Negative thoughts lead to procrastination because they push you to keep putting off the things that you are afraid of taking on. Procrastination then affects your productivity and you become someone who is prone to indecision and inaction. You find that when big moments come you choke and you cannot decide whether to move forward or stay where you are.

The more negative your thoughts are, the more risk-averse and indecisive you will become. When faced with great opportunities, you will balk at the chance to do something different because there is a risk involved. The net result is that you will find your life is going round in circles and that you are not making any progress towards your goals.

In the same way that negative thoughts lead to inaction and procrastination, positive thoughts increase productivity and push you to become proactive. When you are positive you are confident and this means that you are willing to take risks. Hen faced with opportunities or challenges you jump at the chance because your expectation of success is much higher than your expectation of failure.

Positive people know that there is a possibility of failure but they understand that failure is just a normal part of the journey to achieving your goals. This mindset is what causes positive-minded people to have higher risk management toughness and a greater affinity for taking chances. When you are mentally strong, the possibility of failure does not deter you because you understand that failure is part of the process and not the end result.

Until you learn to stop the negative self-dialogue, you will always keep sabotaging your progress by feeding your fear. The more afraid you become to venture out of your comfort zone, the fewer the opportunities that you will be able to identify and seize. Your mind will remain closed off to new ideas and perspectives because anything that challenges your beliefs and identity feels risky and uncomfortable. This means that to overcome the fear of failure you must first embrace a growth mindset.

A mindset refers to the established attitudes and beliefs that you have created over time. People with a fixed mindset believe that their skills, talents, and abilities are predetermined and fixed so they always priorities innate ability over learning. people with fixed mindsets believe that to do something you need to have the natural talent for it or have some sort of pre-existing qualifications.

On the other hand, people who have a growth mindset embrace learning through experiences and challenges. They understand that they have the ability to learn, increase their skills, and aptitudes. They do not look at challenges in terms of how well equipped they are to face them, but rather what they can learn by trying something new. To cultivate a growth mindset you need to open up your mind to learning and changing the way you think.

These two mindsets explain why it is not always the people who are at the top of their class who end up being successful. No matter how high your IQ is, if you do not take a chance on opportunities, challenge yourself and take risks, your brilliance will remain stagnant. On the other hand, people who believe they can increase their skills and abilities by testing and pushing themselves are more likely to get ahead in life because they take risks that the average person would not.

Building a growth mindset where you embrace change and taking risks will help you to build new habits and look at life from a different perspective. A growth mindset helps you to see failure, not as a definition of who you are but as a normal part of learning and growing. To get past the limitations of a fixed mindset prioritize learning and hard work over talent or innate abilities.

There are a lot of talented people who end up doing nothing with their talent because they do not work hard enough. Hard work beats talent if talent does not work hard. Stop worrying about your IQ or what talents or skills you may be lacking and focus on learning by pushing yourself to try new things. Get into the habit of embracing uncertainty and pushing yourself out of the comfort zone you have created. Learn to take risks by taking on challenges and doing something that you would not normally do.

Neuroscience has proven that our brains are plastic. This means that they have the capacity to reorganize and change. Anything that you do not know, you can always learn and any bad habits that you have created can be replaced with good ones. There are no limits to what your brain can learn and unlearn but for this to happen you have to be open to new experiences and change. Do not create limitations on your abilities or your skills. Your skills can grow and you can always find ways to overcome your weaknesses.

People with risk management toughness are not afraid to have flaws, because they know that these flaws are not permanent. If you take failure as an opportunity to learn you will find ways to fix your flaws by learning new things. Instead of avoiding challenges, think of them as a way to discover new 6things about yourself, expand your horizons, and reach your goals.

In overcoming the fear of failure, the most important thing to understand is that fear is internal. It is not caused by the size of the challenge or any other external circumstance. Fear comes from your insecurities, your self-limiting beliefs, and the negative self-dialogue that you engage in constantly. This means that to overcome the fear of failure you need to change how you think about yourself, your abilities, and your beliefs. Before you try and change the situation, first change yourself by questioning your beliefs. Only then will you be able to overcome your insecurities and embrace the uncertainty that comes with taking risks.

The Perfection Fallacy

One of the biggest reasons why people procrastinate and hesitate to take risks is the pursuit of perfection. Perfection is when something comes with all the desired qualities and guarantees in such a way that it is 100% of what you want. Ultimately there is no such thing as perfect in reality because perfection in itself is an idea and so it changes from day to day. What you thought was perfect yesterday may seem flawed today and so in essence the pursuit of perfection is a never-ending mission in futility.

I am sure that you have at some point bought something that you thought was absolutely perfect. The moment you saw it you thought, *this is just perfect, it is everything that I wanted*. Once you get home with your new purchase, the perceived perfection may last a couple of days or even weeks. However sooner or later you start to notice small flaws here and there, get tired of it, and then eventually discard it. This happens often because perfection is an idea, what looks perfect today, will fall short in some way or other tomorrow,

While going for perfection when shopping for goods or services may be a good, albeit somewhat misguided, idea; the pursuit of perfection can become a damaging obsession if you make it a way of life. The perfection fallacy occurs when you start waiting for things to be just "perfect" for you to take action. This means that you are in a constant state of waiting. You are waiting for the perfect job opportunity, waiting for the perfect soulmate, waiting for the perfect market conditions to start a business, the perfect time to start losing weight, and so on.

Of course, since these perfect situations do not exist what you actually end up doing by chasing perfection is nothing worthwhile. People who are always waiting for all their ducks to line up perfectly in a neat row before they can make a move never really get around to doing anything with their lives. They remain stuck in the same situations year in year out because they do not want to take a risk and do something that is not going to be perfect.

One of the biggest hindrances to achieving your goals is an obsession with perfection. It is commonly said that perfection is the enemy of good. This is because perfection keeps you from acting even when there is a clear opportunity ahead of you. You become so afraid of taking chances because you do not want anything to go wrong. The longer you wait, the harder it becomes to act. So you end up just choking at crucial moments and missing out on opportunities to do something great or try something new that could bring you closer to your goals.

Concert pianists, professional athletes, and even theatre performers always keep rehearsing and practicing their craft. This is because they understand that no matter how good you are, there is always room for improvement. So by practicing constantly they get even better at what they do. With each repetition, they get better at what they are good at and they improve on their flaws. Perfectionists miss out on the opportunity to get better and work on their flaws because they do not try at all. For a perfectionist, they want to start at perfect instead of starting at good and working their way up to perfect.

To climb a tree you cannot start from the top, you have to do it bottom-up. The lesson in this simple truth is that to get anywhere you need to start with what you have. You start where you are and gradually build up on the abilities you have, your skills, and your knowledge until you have what you need to achieve your goals and dreams.

You may never end up being perfect. However, when you take a chance and start something, in the end, you will be better than you were when you started. Instead of waiting for things to fall neatly into place, start with what you have and start where you are. As you go along on your journey, you will keep increasing what you have, learning new things, and getting better with each challenge and failure. Some of the most successful people will tell you that the moments in their lives that are most memorable are the ones where they challenged themselves, overcame difficulties, and discovered things about themselves that they never knew.

People who cultivate risk management toughness understand that to get anywhere in life, you must be willing to take the first step. What this means is that sometimes you have to be willing to start with good enough in order to get to what you want. Do not let the illusion of perfection stand in the way of going after your dreams.

There will never be a perfect moment or a perfect opportunity. Unless you take a chance on what is in front of you and work to make it into what you have envisioned, you will always be waiting for an ideal that will never come.

You do not need to have millions of dollars to start a business or just the perfect product or service to become an entrepreneur. Increasingly many businesses have embraced the concept of going to market with a minimum viable product. A minimum viable product is the simplest working version of the product or service that you want to offer. When companies go to market with a minimum viable product, it is not because they are too lazy to finish the product. It is because they want to make improvements to the product based on user feedback and the reaction they get from the consumer.

Imagine if you spent millions of dollars on a product only for you to launch something that consumers just did not want. You would end up having to spend even more to fix the flaws and change the product again. As we have already said perfection is not fixed, it is an idea that shifts from day to day.

The reason behind the success of using a minimum viable product for businesses is that it allows companies to start with what they have. Once they have started with a basic product, they can keep making improvements on it as they learn more and more about what their consumers need. They rely on user feedback as a source of valuable information that they use to fine-tune the product and improve on it until it meets the consumer's needs as best as possible.

You may not be going into business, but having a minimum viable product to start with works in any dimension. It simply means that you start with something good and then fine-tune it and make it better as you go along. The key here is that you start. You do not obsess over the small details, you do not wait for the wind to blow just the right way or any of the other excuses that you use to delay action. Start with your minimum viable product whatever it is and then learn as you go along.

If you want to lose weight, do not wait until you have money to join an expensive weight loss program. Start by making small changes to how you eat and your activity levels. Both of these are free but they will get you started on your journey. When you get too caught up in doing things just a particular way, you may end up wasting valuable time yet you had everything you needed to get started all along.

If you want to start a business you do not need to have millions in capital. Plenty of successful businesses started in people's basements as they worked to build up their capital. If you are determined to see your goal through, then you will not let the little inconveniences and details stand in your way. Most of the time we use perfection as an excuse to delay action because we are afraid to take risks or push ourselves out of the safety of our comfort zone.

If you never try, you will never know what you could have achieved. Your dreams will gather dust in a drawer somewhere as you wait for just the perfect moment to act or get moving. Build your risk management toughness by embracing uncertainty and getting over procrastination. Train yourself to take the first step. Most people find that once they take the first step, then the rest of the steps are not so hard to take.

Break down your goals into smaller steps that will help you to focus on the process instead of the result. Stop wondering whether the outcome will be a success or not and simply commit to what you need to do today. When you build discipline and invest in the process the results will take care of themselves. Any good baker will tell you that it is the preparation that makes or breaks the cake. So, all their energy and focus are usually on the preparation process. Once the cake's in the oven there is little, they can do to change the outcome.

All this means is that worrying about perfection does not add any value to your outcome. Your efforts and energy should be on the actions you can take now to ensure the outcome that you want. The outcome may not be perfect but it will always be better than staying stuck in the same situation because you are busy waiting for things to be just right before you make a move.

Risk takers are not bold because they know the outcome that is waiting for them down the pike. Rather, they get their confidence from knowing that if they keep doing the right thing consistently sooner or later, they will get where they need to go. Trust in the process and let it guide you to the result you want. At the end of it all, whether you succeed or fail, you will still be a better person than you were when you started.

Beating Procrastination

How often do you put off certain tasks and important decisions? We are all susceptible to procrastination from time to time. Sometimes you simply do not feel like doing something because it is boring and you would rather do something else. Sometimes you do not know how to do it, so you keep putting it off. Other times you are too overwhelmed and simply cannot find the time to do it.

Most times you put things off because you are afraid you will fail or do something wrong.

Ultimately it does not matter why you procrastinate. Whether it is good old laziness or something deeper, the net result of procrastination is the same; inaction. Procrastination hinders productivity and can be the biggest hindrance to you achieving your goals. If you keep putting things off, what eventually happens is that you end up doing things that do not really matter because you are avoiding doing the things that are difficult or challenging.

Many people do not realize how much time they lose due to procrastination. The more they put off things, the more ingrained this habit becomes. You will often find people who are always running behind on their deadlines, falling behind on their work, and missing out on opportunities constantly. These are people who always wait until the last minute when they no longer have a choice but to get things done.

If you fall into the habit of always doing things last minute, you will be in a perpetual state of anxiety. People who procrastinate are always playing catch-up because they need to make up for all the time they lose by procrastinating and putting things off.

Most procrastinators tend to have one thing in common. They lack sufficient self-discipline to regulate their emotions. If you stop to think about it, you will realize that most of the times that you put things off, it is because of some emotional resistance. Either you do not feel motivated enough, or you want to do something less difficult or you are afraid to fail. In all these cases your emotions cause you to procrastinate.

When you cannot regulate your emotions, they tend to become the driving force behind your actions. You will choose pleasure over hard work even if it means not achieving your goal. You will seek instant gratification because you want to feel good. Emotions are powerful motivators and unfortunately most of the emotional decisions we make end up being our own undoing. This is why it is almost impossible to cultivate mental toughness without self-discipline.

If your ability to regulate your emotions cannot overcome your impulses then you will often find yourself avoiding things that you know you should be doing. It is natural to want to feel good but you need to understand that sometimes you need to postpone the reward in order to get things done. When you get into a habit of avoiding anything difficult or challenging you will not be able to tap into your real potential because all you will be doing is skating through life.

To achieve anything worthwhile, you must be willing to work for it and persevere through inconveniences. You cannot base your actions and habits on emotions and moods but rather you need to overcome your urges and learn to focus on what is important. For example, if you are a student, you may sometimes feel like studying is getting in the way of you having fun. However, if you stop to consider what is at stake, you will realize which of the two activities will matter to your long term goals and your future.

Getting over the need for instant gratification may not be the easiest thing to do but if you can train yourself to do a cost-benefit analysis, the things you should prioritize will become pretty obvious. If you do not feel like going to the gym and just want to lounge on your couch, weigh the momentary pleasure of one hour on the couch against the cost of being overweight and unhealthy. Obviously in the long run your health is too high a price to pay for a few minutes of pleasure.

By considering what is at stake, you move away from making decisions based on emotions to making decisions that are founded on logic. If you can make this a habit especially when making important decisions and taking on challenging tasks, you will find that you procrastinate less and less. Consider each choice with its possible long term consequences. This kind of analysis will help you to get some perspective on what is important and what is simply a distraction.

Another simple way to beat procrastination is by investing in schedules, timetables, and deliberate actions. If you are a writer, for example, and you only write when inspiration strikes, chances are your productivity is pretty low. This is because tying your actions to emotions leaves a lot of room for inaction. However if you instead of waiting for motivation, commit to writing a certain number of words each day, then your productivity will naturally go up.

When you create plans of actions and schedules that keep you committed to doing certain things consistently, you effectively make taking action the only option. This eliminates the tendency to be indecisive and to procrastinate. In such a case it is your self-discipline that will prompt you to get things done and keep you dedicated to achieving your goals.

Come up with to-do lists that have clear schedules and plans of actions of what you need to do each day, each week, and so on. The more you repeat these deliberate actions consistently, they will gradually turn into habits, Habits will eventually become a way of life and in this way, you will have created a sure path to your goals.

Think of the kind of rigorous training navy seals go through. They do not practice when they feel like or when the circumstances are just right. Instead, they commit to set schedules and time tables that ensure that they consistently do what they need to do regardless of the circumstances. This prioritization of self-discipline is what leads to the development of habits and creates a clear path to your goals.

Do not leave your outcomes up to fate or luck or other people. When you make plans of action, you are literally taking control of your outcomes by ensuring that you are doing the things that will help you achieve your goals. Instead of banking on motivation and inspiration to get you moving, invest in good habits, schedules, and concrete plans of action.

Chapter 9: Navy Seal Strategies for Mental Toughness and Self-discipline

Sheer endurance, determination, and the ability to persevere through extreme hardships are just some of the qualities that set navy seals apart from any of the other disciplined forces. This elite group of soldiers cultivate extraordinary levels of discipline and focus that are built on mental toughness. Only a select few individuals make it through the Navy Seal training because it goes beyond just physical endurance to mental strength and resilience.

While physical endurance may be difficult to achieve, it is the mental toughness that poses a challenge for most people. Most of our beliefs and attitudes start with how we think so naturally before you can build any kind of endurance or resilience, you must first believe that you can. This requires not just self-belief but extraordinary levels of discipline that enable you to dedicate yourself fully to a particular mission or goal.

You may not be planning to join the seals or go to battle any time soon. However, without self-discipline and mental toughness, your goals will always be just out of reach. This is because it is not enough to just have a goal. You also need a plan of action on how you will achieve this goal. Once you have a plan of action you need to commit to it and follow through on it regardless of how you feel or what the circumstances are. These are the invaluable lessons that you can take from the navy seals and use them to help you to reach your goals and stay on track.

When most people fail it is not due o lack of vision or plans. It is because they lack the self-discipline to be consistent in their actions until they get to their goals. In most cases, you will start something with a lot of energy and motivation. You will be very conscientious about it early on. However, as the motivation you feel starts to wane with time, you will start to lose your consistency. Your actions will become erratic and haphazard instead of deliberately.

Slowly something that meant so much to you, in the beginning, starts to lose its appeal because it has become too challenging. This kind of trajectory is what makes it so hard for so many people to see their goals through to the end. They will only pursue their goals while it is convenient and easy to do so. The minute they start running into challenges and obstacles, then their emotional resistance kicks in and they start to look for shortcuts or an easy way out.

Without discipline and the ability to overcome emotional impulses, perseverance and grit will remain nothing but words. This is why aiming for the kind of discipline that navy seals cultivate may be the kick in the ass that you need to actively start going after your dreams. The kind of discipline that navy seals have is something that people can learn and use in their daily lives to develop the mental strength that they need to pursue their goals.

Mental strength is a trait that you can cultivate and develop so anyone no matter what they do or how old they are can learn to be more resilient. Most of the time you give up on a goal when you are just about to reach the finish line because that's when the mental fatigue sets in.

Your motivation fails you because it is a fleeting emotion that comes and goes depending on your circumstances. Unless you have self-discipline to fall back on when motivation wanes, you will be left with nothing to keep you committed to your goals. To overcome mental exhaustion and emotional fatigue you need mental toughness to enable you to persevere and stay dedicated to your goals even in unfavorable and daunting circumstances.

One of the ways in which people increase their mental strength is by investing in the process and focusing on the deliberate steps they need to take each day. One of the reasons why motivation tends to wane is that usually we are motivated by the end result and not the process. Naturally, when the process becomes difficult and unpleasant, this motivation starts to fade because it was centered on the results without bearing in mind the process that you will have to go through to get to the results.

When you learn to value the process, you do not give up easily because it is not all about the result. This is what the navy seals do to build perseverance and stay committed to their mission no matter how extenuating the circumstances are. Navy seals commit themselves 100% to the process because they understand that if you get the process right then you will get the result you want by default.

Push Yourself

When you are flailing and you simply cannot find the extra strength to go on, how do you keep going? For the navy seals, they push themselves by considering what is at stake. Navy seals have to be good at what they do because they know that one mistake could cost them their lives. This is what gives them the mental strength to push beyond exhaustion and failure to find that last inner reserve of strength that they need to persevere.

When you feel that you simply just do not have the strength or will to persevere, ask yourself what is at stake. What do you stand to lose by giving up on your dreams because you are too tired, or too afraid? For JK Rowling who was rejected 12 times, she kept going back time and time again because her dream was at stake. When something you have worked for all your life is in jeopardy then naturally you will do everything in your power to keep the dream alive.

The best way to push yourself is by always reminding yourself what success will mean to you. What will you gain by achieving your goal and seeing your dream come to life? Often when you lose your commitment and dedication it is because you have lost sight of what you wanted to achieve in the first place. No matter how difficult the road gets, always remind yourself why you started in the first place.

The more you are able to see the bigger picture, the more endurance you will have to help you get past the challenges and the hard times. People are willing to go to extraordinary lengths if what is at stake is more important than the fear of failure. Always look at the cost of winning as the price you have to pay to realize your dream. So if the price is getting back up twelve times after being rejected time and time again then make that sacrifice because the thirteenth time could be the one time that your goal becomes reality.

Start by asking yourself what is at stake if you do not keep going. Is it your career, your marriage, your health, or your financial freedom? Whatever it is, always have that in the back of your mind before you make a decision. Make the stakes high enough that the only acceptable option is to keep going. Imagine what it will mean if you actually reach that goal versus what it will mean if you do not. Having a clear grasp of the consequence of both action and inaction is one of the best ways to push yourself to keep going even when you do not feel like.

Look down the pike, five years from now. Will you still be at the same dead-end job because you are too afraid to go back to college and get that degree? Two years from now will you be divorced and out of touch with your children because you do not want to work on your marriage? In one year will you be dealing with multiple health issues because losing weight is too hard? Whatever is at stake for you, should be your reason to never quit. Try as many times as you need to until you get it right.

The one thing that navy seals always know is that failure is not an option. The stakes are too high and the consequence of not getting it right will be more painful than any training that they have to endure. Whatever the stakes are for you, take failure out of the equation and leave yourself no option but to persevere until you get the desired outcome.

Whenever you start to feel disillusioned, doubtful, or afraid just ask yourself what is at stake, and can I really afford to give up? Somewhere in that answer, you will find the strength that you need to keep going.

Adapt and Keep It Moving

Navy seals make a habit of bouncing back from the unexpected. In their line of work, they do not have the luxury of knowing what is going to happen beforehand. All they can do is prepare and get be ready for anything. That is why they are so dedicated to their training. Things can go from peaceful to life-threatening in a split second. If they lack mental strength in such a situation, they will not be able to survive.

In developing mental toughness one of the most important skills you will require is resilience or the ability to bounce back from failure. In life, you cannot be sure about a whole lot of things. However, the one thing that you can be sure of is that there will always be setbacks and challenges in your path. This is why without resilience, giving up becomes a way of life because you will always falter at the first sign of trouble.

Life rarely if ever, unfolds as we planned or expected. Every day things change and all the best-laid plans can go up in smoke because of something you never saw coming. When you set out your goals, it is crucial to understand that you may have to change your plan from time to time, you may have to change who you are and you may even have to try a different route to get to your destination. This flexibility and adaptability are key factors in becoming resilient and developing mental toughness.

Bouncing back from failure is an integral part of succeeding. Expecting that things will go your way automatically on the first try is delusional. You have to be willing to go the distance even when the unexpected happens and your plan is no longer working. This capacity to adapt is what will determine how well and how quickly you get back up on your feet after failing. Some people are so obstinate and stuck in their beliefs and attitudes that they are incapable of adjusting their attitudes even if it means learning something new in the process.

Think of someone who had just put all of their life savings into a business just before the global pandemic hit. They had done all their homework, come up with impeccable market research, and laid the foundation for a successful business. Suddenly, life was brought to a standstill by a global pandemic that put everything on lockdown. No matter how well prepared you are, the unexpected can still happen. They will always be things that you cannot control. In such situations giving up seems like the only way out because you have no control over what is happening.

If you take time to learn from the navy seal's training, you will find that overcoming and bouncing back when you are blind-sighted is one of the key elements of mental strength. Everyone can stay up on their feet when they are not facing any challenges or setbacks. The real test of mental toughness is what you do when things go wrong and you have to start again from scratch. What do you do when things suddenly spiral out of control? Do you go down and stay down or do you claw your way back up?

Navy seals encounter the unexpected often so they have trained themselves to bounce back even when they are caught off guard. They do not stand around looking for something or someone to blame or start complaining about how unfair life is. They acknowledge the problem, adapt to the new situation, and continue on their mission. This is what resilience is all about acceptance and adapting to the situation that you find yourself in.

If you cannot pursue your goals unless everything goes exactly according to your plan, then you will end up not achieving any of your goals. Life has no guarantees to offer anyone so the pursuit of your goals should not be tied to things staying in your favor or your path being obstacle-free. Train yourself to be adaptable and resilient in such a way that whatever happens your goal remains the same, it is only your strategy and tactics that need to be adapted to the situation.

When you make decisions and plans, always make them with the expectation that at some point you may have to face something you did not plan for. Expect and accept that change is inevitable and that the only way to go through it is by adapting.

Another lesson we can learn from the navy seals is that they do not waste time on things that they cannot change. This is a valuable lesson because most people waste a lot of time focusing on the circumstances instead of building themselves and their strength. If you have to go into battle you do not waste precious time counting the enemy, you use that energy to improve your own capacity to win by training yourself and getting yourself ready.

When you encounter the unexpected, do not get caught up in trying to change things that are out of your control. Look for things that you can change and use those to adapt to the situation. A good example of people who focused on what they could control is the businesses that turned to online operations when the global pandemic hit. They realized that they had no control over the pandemic, but that they could change was the way they operated to be able to function in a lockdown. This kind of resilience is what it means to bounce back from the unexpected and keep it moving.

Every day find ways to pivot and adapt to changes that come your way. The more adaptable you are the better you will be at recognizing opportunities and seizing them. Every unexpected occurrence that comes your way carries challenges and opportunities in equal measure. Whether you see one or the other will ultimately come down to your ability to bounce back and adapt to change.

Visualize your Success

Navy seals are trained to always visualize themselves completing their mission successfully. By doing this they prime their minds for success which helps to make the goal clearer and easy to focus on. If you are to achieve mental toughness, one of the ways to do this is to make a habit of visualizing the accomplishment of your goal.

When you can see the outcome of the goal, and experience what the accomplishment of the goal will feel like from the onset, then everything standing in your way becomes manageable. Having a clear mental picture of what your success will mean can turn even the biggest obstacles into minor inconveniences. The first step in perseverance is understanding that whatever it is that you are aiming for is within your reach. This is why visualization is so important. It makes your goal seem real and tangible.

Research has found that people who use vision boards are more likely to reach their goals than people who do not. A vision board serves as a physical reminder of what you are aiming for and gives you a glimpse of what your goal will look like when actualized. This is one of the ways that you can keep yourself committed and dedicated to achieving your goal.

Some people find that putting a picture of themselves when they were fit or of someone whose body they admire on their fridge helps them to eat healthier and stay on track in terms of fitness goals. This kind of visualization works because your goal is not something far off in the distance but something that you can look at and find motivation in. Physical reminders of your goal are powerful but so is mental visualization. Even taking some time each morning to visualize what you want to achieve can have an incredible mental impact on your confidence and ability to face challenges.

If you are having a hard time staying on course or you are tempted to give up, keep a physical representation of what you want to achieve close by to give you a glimpse of what you will gain if you keep pressing on. Alternatively, close your eyes and visualize achieving your goal. Picture every detail vividly and let that image stay in your mind. By preparing your mind for the win, you effectively equip yourself to deal with any obstacles that may come your way.

Self-Affirmation

Navy seals have a creed that says, "*I will not quit. I persevere and thrive in adversity. If knocked down, I will get back up. Every time. I am never out of the fight.*" This creed is not just self-affirming but boosts confidence and gives the seals the mental strength to persevere through difficulties and challenges.

What thoughts do you have running in a continuous loop in your mind? Are they self-affirming and positive or are they negative and self-critical? If your thoughts and your internal dialogue are always negative and tainted with self-doubt how can you find the mental strength required to persevere and overcome obstacles?

Thoughts become reality and the more often you say things like *I can't, it's too difficult, I am tired*, and so on, the more difficult it becomes to achieve your goals. People who are mentally strong use their thoughts to cheer themselves on and not to sabotage themselves. You may not be aware of it but all the negative things you say to yourself have a big impact on your self-esteem and confidence. That is why sometimes you find that you talk yourself out of opportunities because you keep focusing on the negative until you no longer have the courage to seize the opportunity.

A positive mindset opens your mind up to possibilities and provides you with the mental strength that you need to see things through. If, for instance, you are going through your workout routine and listening to an upbeat song you are likely to feel energized and up to the challenge. However, if you decide to put on some slow, boring music, you will likely bring your energy down and end up either quitting halfway or not starting at all.

To understand self-affirmation, think of your thoughts as the soundtrack to your life that is playing in your mind. Is it spurring you on and making you feel confident or is it tearing down even the little confidence that you have? Be careful of the thoughts that you allow to become dominant in your mind. This means being more mindful and present. As you go about your day, question your thoughts, what are your thoughts focused on? Are they positive or are they negative?

The problem with negative thinking is that it tends to become a habit. You find yourself always criticizing yourself, focusing on your weaknesses, and bringing yourself down. Most people who quit do not do it because someone else told them to. They quit because they have managed to convince themselves that they will not succeed. When you feel negative thoughts start to overwhelm you and cloud your judgment always ask yourself, *Would I say things like this to my best friend or someone I love*? If you wouldn't, then why are you saying them to yourself?

Practice self-empathy by being kind to yourself. You would never say things like *you are so stupid, you are too fat, you are a failure...* to someone else yet for some people this is what they are constantly telling themselves. Look for ways to cheer yourself on and not drag yourself down. Focus on the positive and what you are good at. Everybody makes mistakes and flogging yourself with your past over and over again is not going to change what happened.

Look for positive affirmations and mantras that boost your courage and your confidence. Affirmations such as, *I am talented, I am confident and I can do this...* or *this is just a test, I will not quit...* are simple but effective mantras you can repeat to yourself daily to help you stay positive.

You always have a choice you can choose to be your own best friend, find ways to be positive, and build yourself up or you can choose to be self-critical, negative, and tear yourself down. Whichever one you pick, will determine whether or not your goals become reality or simply things that you wish you had done.

Keep Your Eyes on the Ball

It is amazing what you can accomplish when you are focused and committed. Often when you are distracted, your mind is all over the place and you keep missing important details because your mind is on other things. Navy seals are trained to have an unwavering focus on their goal no matter what is going on around them. They are trained that the most important thing is their mission and everything that they do should be focused on the realization of that goal.

For most people staying focused is the real challenge when it comes to mental toughness. They may start with the best intentions but halfway through the journey they get distracted and lose sight of what they were aiming for. Think of it this way, distractions occupy mental space and by so doing diminish the amount of mental energy that you can devote to your goals or the things that are really important.

In much the same way that multi-tasking diminishes brain efficacy, distractions will affect your ability to stay committed and dedicated to your goal. Some people try to pursue so many things all at once that at the end of it all they end up achieving none of them. Having a clear focus is the only way to ensure that your mind, time, and energy are not being wasted on things that do not really matter. Identify what your key goals are and make them your point of focus.

Consider what happens when you are working and your phone keeps ringing. Every time you have to stop what you are doing and answer it, you lose sight of what you were doing and eventually you start thinking about other things instead of the task at hand. Research indicates that multitasking reduces brain efficiency. This is because your brain only has so much energy and space to go around. The more things that you pack in there, the less space it has for the important things. This means that to achieve your goals, you must be able to recognize and overcome distractions.

Distractions can easily make you forget what your main aim was and divert your attention from important matters. You will find that people who went to school aiming to pass and get into good colleges, will halfway through their journey get caught up in popularity contests and lose sight of their goals. People who joined a company aiming to ascend to management suddenly spend most of their energy trying to sabotage that one person who they perceive to be competition. When this happens, the inevitable outcome is that other things become more important than your goal and before you realize it, you cannot even remember what it is that you wanted in the first place.

Having the bigger picture always in your mind will help you to understand which battles are worth fighting and which ones are simply wasting your time. Always ask yourself, *if I do this will it help me to achieve what I want?* If the answer is no, then you are better off not doing it at all.

Ultimately, mental toughness is an inside job. You have to make a conscious decision to commit and dedicate yourself to making things happen in order to get what you want. Mentally strong people skew the odds in their favor through discipline and deliberate actions. They investing in habits and routines that make the stay on the path to achieving their goals and realizing their dreams.

Chapter 10: What Does Mental Strength Look Like

Your mental strength is not tested when everything is going smoothly. Rather, your resilience and grit are the things you discover about yourself when the shit hit the fan. In the moments when giving up seems like the only option, when there is no visible light at the end of the tunnel and you are mentally and physically exhausted; that is when your mental strength is tested.

Being resilient does not mean that you enjoy hardships or that disappointment does not hit you as hard as it does the average person. It simply means that you handle tough situations better because you have cultivated a growth mindset that allows you to see beyond failure. Most of the time when you give up, it is because you feel like there is no possible way to overcome whatever difficulty or challenge your facing. This is why mental strength requires you to change the way you react to difficulty.

Resilience and grit will not make you immune to hardships. However, they will equip you to get through hardships and obstacles without losing sight of your goals or the bigger picture. Often, we come across people who seem indestructible. They go through bankruptcies, divorces, job loss and a myriad of other disappoints yet they still manage to get back on their feet and reinvent themselves. To understand how these mentally strong people are able to go about life unfazed by challenges or failure, it is important to understand what exactly mental strength looks like.

Ten Things That Mentally Strong People Do Not Do

1. Mentally strong people do not generalize

Mentally strong people do not view failure as a continuous event. When people generalize, they get into a habit of thinking in absolutes. Thoughts such as, *I never get things right, I always fail at Math, this always happens to me,* are generalizations that can affect your ability to see things objectively. When you generalize you have already given yourself permission to fail since you have a belief that you have created about the challenge you are facing.

Mentally strong people do not generalize because they do not judge their present using past experiences. They learn to view failure as a singular event and not a way of life. Consider how many times you hesitate or avoid doing something altogether because in the past it did not go so well for you. Maybe you botched a proposal so you decided you suck at presentations and always sit them out, or you crashed out of a weight loss program so you decided you cannot lose weight.

So often we take failure and use it to define who we are, what we can and cannot do, and even what opportunities we should or should not go after. In contrast, mentally strong people do not let past mistakes dictate what they can and cannot do. In fact, they use failure as a lesson to inform their actions the next time around. Mentally strong people figure that next time they will know *what not to do* so they have a higher chance of success. To build resilience and grit, you have to do what mentally strong people do; stop generalizing and judge each situation objectively.

2. Mentally strong people do not catastrophize

Making mountains out of molehills is one of the surest ways to talk yourself out of going after your dreams. Mentally strong people do not catastrophize. When you get into a habit of viewing every challenge as an opportunity for failure then chances are you are constantly afraid of moving forward. Catastrophizing is when you turn everything into a big deal.

People with a tendency to catastrophize tend to magnify challenges until they take on larger than life proportions. Even simple tasks start to seem like a test of their self-worth and abilities. When you approach everything like it is a life and death situation, then do not be surprised if you constantly feel overwhelmed and tempted to quit. Mentally strong people know how to put things in perspective. They understand that no situation will alter the course of their entire lives unless they allow it to.

It may be a cliché but the truth in the statement what does not kill you makes you stronger is hard to ignore. Failure often opens up our eyes and compels us to do better. It is an essential part of any success story and this is why mentally strong people view failure as nothing but a minor bump on the road. Mentally strong people adopt the attitude of *what is the worst that can happen?* When you adopt this kind of thinking, you will realize that things are not always as bad as they seem and there is always an opportunity to redeem yourself if things do not go your way.

3. Mentally strong people do not throw pity parties.

Mentally strong people do not dwell on their mistakes or their circumstances. They understand that the only way to get past failure is to keep moving. If you spend too much time dwelling on your mistakes, or your weaknesses you will become more focused on your past as opposed to your future. No one ever gets forward by looking forward. Your focus and energize should be on what you can do now to have better outcomes tomorrow.

Most people give up because they cannot see past the situation there are in. To move forward you must stop feeling sorry for yourself and focus on the next step. When you come across mentally strong people you may think they do not have any challenges in their life. This is because they are always talking about their plans, what they are working towards, and what they hope to achieve. Mentally strong people do not waste time lamenting or complaining about their lives. This is because they understand the future is not in what happened in the past but rather what they can make happen.

Fixating on your mistakes or your failures only makes you blind to opportunities and undermines your confidence. Resist the urge to indulge in self-pity and waste time complaining about how unfair life is. If there is one thing that mentally strong people understand, it is that nothing happens until you make a move. The more focused you are on the past, the harder it is to move forward.

4. Mentally strong people do not make emotional decisions

Mentally strong people are not hostage to their emotions or impulses. They understand that when you base your actions and decisions on moods, then your consistency and commitment suffer. Mentally strong people are just like you. They also experience emotions both negative and positive. They also have days when they feel down in the dumps and mentally exhausted. However, mentally strong people are able to self-regulate because even when they feel these negative emotions, they have a plan of action.

Just like Navy seals who cultivate self-discipline to help them stay focused, mentally strong people take emotion out of the equation by investing in plans and systems. It can be as simple as leaving your work out gear out each night so it's the first thing you see in the morning. Or, making a to-do list each day when you get to the office to have a clear schedule of what you need to do.

By taking deliberate action, moods stop being the reason why you do things. Mentally strong people do not wait for motivation or inspiration to strike. They stick to plans, schedules, and time tables because they understand that emotions are fleeting while discipline is not. Mentally strong people understand that to reach their goals, they need to be consistent and deliberate. They use discipline to stay on track and commit to a process that does not depend on what mood they are in that day.

5. Mentally strong people do not feed their fear

*What if I fail, what if I am not qualified, what if I screw it up...*The what-if game is one that people play often. The only purpose this kind of thinking serves is to feed your fear and undermine your confidence. Mentally strong people do not feed their fear because they know the impact that negative self-talk has on their ability to go after their dreams.

How often do you talk yourself out of doing something by constantly thinking of all the things that could go wrong? When you are constantly feeding your fear by amplifying the possibility of failure, do not be surprised if you become prone to procrastination. Fear is one of the most powerful motivators known to man and unfortunately, most times fear makes you incapable of moving forward.

Mentally strong people understand that when they focus on the positives, they can effectively stop feeding their fear. The less you dwell on the possibility of failure the less power your fear has over you. If you can approach challenges as an opportunity to possibly succeed or learn something new, you will not be paralyzed by fear every time you are facing a difficult situation.

Mentally strong people replace negative emotions such as fear with positive ones by focusing on their strengths. Ultimately negative emotions are fed by negative thoughts so if you can change your self-talk, then you can change fear into hope and enthusiasm.

6. Mentally strong people do not overthink
Nothing makes you more prone to inaction and self-doubt than overthinking. If you spend every waking moment over-analyzing, dissecting, and ruminating over every little detail, chances are you will be constantly overwhelmed and unsure of yourself. Overthinking takes your focus and energy from what you should be doing and diverts it to worry.

Mentally strong people spend less time thinking and more time doing. They do not succumb to the urge to over-process information or obsess over the small details. The more time you spend thinking the less time you have to act. Mentally strong people understand that action inspires confidence and keeps them moving forward so they focus on getting things done.

A mentally strong person will not spend hours trying to analyze what their boss meant when they criticized them or why a colleague was aloof in the break room. All their energy is on what they need to do because they understand overthinking does not really solve anything.

7. Mentally strong people do not waste time on things they cannot control

Fretting over other people's opinions, traffic, economic downturns and all the other hundreds of things beyond your control is not just an exercise in futility but a waste of time and energy. Mentally strong people stay on track by focusing on what they can control. They understand that their power lies in the things they have control over so they invest their time and energy on their own efforts.

Spending time and energy trying to get people to like you or worrying about what things beyond your control is counterproductive. People who are mentally strong have a razor focus on their goals and what they need to achieve them. They understand that they only have so much energy and time so if they waste it on distractions, then they are less likely to reach their goals.

How many people get so caught up in office politics or trying to impress people that they forget to actually do their job? A mentally strong person knows what is important in terms of the bigger picture and what is merely a distraction. They are not reactive in nature so they do not let circumstances or other people influence their behavior. Mentally strong people do what they need to regardless of what is going on around them. This kind of consistency and commitment to one's goals is what makes the difference between people who are able to achieve the extraordinary and those who get lost somewhere along the way.

8. Mentally strong people do not let their circumstances define them

Mentally strong people are not concerned with labels or what the odds are. they do not go around thinking, *I am just a nerd*, or *I come from the wrong background* or *I do not fit in*. They understand that if your dedicated and committed to your goals then where you are coming from has little to do with how far you can go.

It is common to get into the habit of putting labels on yourself based on your past. This kind of labeling is not just self-limiting but it also puts you in a small limited box where your abilities are limited by your beliefs and ideas about who you are. Think of a student who walks into class each day thinking, *I am the odd one out here, I do not belong.* With this kind of thinking they will probably not do well because they have already put themselves at the back of the race mentally.

Mentally strong people are not bogged down by details such as where they came from, who they know, or what they have. They understand that what they can do is more important so they waste no time on labels or stereotypes. They simply focus on their goals and let their efforts determine what they can and cannot do. Do not allow yourself to be held back by the ideas you have about who you are or what you are supposed to be. The only limits on your potential are the ones that you create for yourself.

9. Mentally strong people do not compare themselves with others

Constantly comparing yourself with others, resenting other people's success, and feeling like you always have to win by bringing other people down are all classic signs of lack of mental strength. Mentally strong people are comfortable in their own skin and they perfect the art of staying in their lane. A mentally strong person runs their own race because they understand that everyone has their own goals and we all get to them at our own pace.

When you are consumed with trying to keep up with other people or show them up, it distracts you from what is really important. To stay focused you need to identify what is important to you and then go after it. When you get so busy comparing your life with others or trying to be like someone else, you lose sight of your own goals. Your objectives should be things that are meaningful and important to you and not a way of trying to keep up with other people.

When your goals are not really your own but a reflection of other people's, your passion towards them will not be strong enough to keep you committed. Do not try to live your life by other people's standards because their goals and yours are not identical. Embrace your uniqueness, do not be afraid to stand out and most importantly carve out your own path that helps you to stay true to who you are.

10. Mentally strong people do not shy away from risks

Mentally strong people understand that to get extraordinary results you must be willing to do something out of the ordinary. Insanity is aptly described as doing the same thing and expecting different results. That is why mentally strong people are quick to adapt to change and try new things. They do not shy away from risks because they understand that with great rewards comes great risk.

Stop trying to tow the safe line in an attempt to avoid failure. When you become so risk-averse that you cannot take a chance on something new, you will never go beyond average. People who take chances have access to more opportunities and these opportunities bring them closer to their goals. Make a commitment to yourself to always do something you have never done. Even if it does not work out, you still get to learn something about yourself that you did not know before.

Mentally strong people embrace uncertainty because they have enough self-belief to know that whatever comes down the pike, they will be able to handle it. Just as it is not possible to fish from the shore, sometimes you must be willing to take risks to get the things you want. Ultimately mental strength is about having the courage to go after what you want no matter what the circumstances are.

The Systemic Approach to Mental Strength

Cultivating mental strength is not something that you do once or twice. Rather it takes consistent steps to make changes in your life and build habits that keep you on course to realizing your goals. This means that achieving mental strength comes down to the small deliberate actions that you take each day. When you cultivate mental strength as a way of life then habits like procrastination, overthinking and inaction are gradually eliminated from your life.

Control your environment

We rarely take time to think about what kind of environments we function in. However, research has shown that a conducive environment may have a positive impact on productivity and increase our overall efficiency when it comes to getting things done. This means that the kind of environment you work in can have a great impact on your ability to stay focused. To build your mental strength, take time to create the right atmosphere and work environment.

Distractions such as cellphones, clutter, and even busy work can keep you from doing what you need to do. The trouble with distractions is that they overwhelm you and take your focus away from the important goals you need to be working on. That is why mentally strong people take charge of their environments and create a workspace that keeps distractions to a minimum. This means staying organized and avoiding clutter both physically and mentally.

When you have mental clutter, it means that you are trying to do too much at once and this inevitably reduces your efficiency. People who multitask often find that they have a lot of half-finished projects or things that never really see the light of day. This is because you only have so much time and energy to work with. If you spread yourself too thin, you will end up having to give up on some things because you simply do not have the time and energy for them.

It is important to control your environment in such a way that it does not hinder your productivity and efficiency. Make it a point to declutter both mentally and physically. The less you have to contend with, the easier it will be to focus on the things that are really important. Remember being mentally strong does not mean that you will not face obstacles. Rather it means that you will be better prepared to handle them when they crop up.

Be More Mindful

Being mindful means being more present in your life. This means switching off the autopilot, reducing the mental experiences, and tuning in to what is actually going on in your life in the moment. A lot of times our worries and fears are driven by thoughts of the past or worries about the future. When you are disconnected from your present, it is easy to miss opportunities because your mind is always on what happened or what may happen.

Mindfulness teaches you to live in the moment and this is one of the most effective ways to cultivate mental strength. When you do not judge situations based on past mistakes then you become less susceptible to the fear of failure. Being mindful frees you from the emotional baggage that makes you have negative thoughts about situations and possible outcomes. When you live in the present, the past has no hold over you and you can focus on your energy on what you need to do today.

Being mindful and present gives you back control over your life by bringing your focus back to the now. Most of the anxiety and stress you feel is linked to what you think will happen or the mistakes you may have made in the past. When you can effectively ditch these worries and simply focus on what is going on in your life, you will free yourself from unnecessary negativity and emotional baggage.

Imagine how freeing it would be to be able to approach situations objectively without trying to compare everything with what happened in the past. How much more confident would you be if every step you take was not tinged with worry about what will happen tomorrow? The thing you need to realize about procrastination is that it is not so much about the task at hand but rather the fear and the uncertainty that gets you.

To be more mindful and present enables you to be more invested in the process and not overly preoccupied with the result. Being present means that you can dedicate yourself to doing what you need to today and let the future unfold as it will. Mindfulness is not just a great way to beat stress and anxiety but it will also help you overcome indecision and inaction.

Simple tips for mindfulness:

- Meditation is a great way to bring your mind back to the present and ground yourself in what is happening in the moment
- Exercise is one of the easiest ways to get out of your own head. Simply going for a walk or a jog can help you refocus your mind and get rid of mental experiences.
- Journaling is a simple but effective technique for being more present in your life. There is something about writing things down that helps you stay in touch with your thoughts and emotions.
- Listen to your thoughts. You would be surprised at how many times we operate on autopilot or from habit. Learn to question your beliefs and motives. Before you make a decision ask yourself why you feel the way you do.
- Put a timer on the worry. Allocate a fixed amount of time to go over whatever is plaguing then make a decision after the time allocated has lapsed. This will help you to avoid overthinking and spending too much time on one thing.

Focus on the things that you can change

If you want to spend more time doing and less time thinking, you need to focus on the things that you can change. Most of our worry stems from things that we cannot control. This preoccupation with external circumstances makes us feel helpless and inadequate. To overcome procrastination, you first need to stop giving control of your life to others or to external circumstances. Do not waste time worrying about what your boss will think, or if the customer will be in a good mood or whatever else you are worrying about that is not in your control. Instead, put all of your focus on your role and whatever it is that you need to do.

If you study for your exam adequately and get most of the answers right then it really will not matter whether the teacher likes you or not. If you make an outstanding pitch then it will hit home regardless of what mood the client is in. Your power lies in what you can control and not in the actions of others. Procrastinators get intimidated by the circumstances and they forget to focus on their strengths. When you choose to be driven by your passion, your goals, and your dreams then the circumstances are nothing more than a blip on your radar. Keeping your focus on what is within your control means you have less time to worry. Invest in your outcome by doing your part regardless of what the circumstances are.

Take the emotion out of it

To make it easier for you to stay on track regardless of what you are thinking or feeling, you need to invest in schedules and deliberate plans. When you have a schedule it does not say, I will do this if I am in the mood, or I will do this when I feel motivated. A schedule tells you to do certain things at certain times. This leaves little room for procrastination because your actions are not dependent on emotions. When you have a plan, it means that you have committed to doing something at a certain time and within a certain time frame. Schedules and plans help you to cultivate the self-discipline that you need to get past emotional resistance. Something as simple as having a prioritized to-do list each day can significantly improve your productivity. Learn to prioritize and write down the things that you need to do each day. At the end of the day go through your list and check that you did everything you were supposed. It may seem simple but having a to-do list gives you a clear plan of action and keeps you accountable to yourself.

Conclusion

The capacity of the human brain to reorganize itself is amazing. It gives us the capacity to unlearn bad habits and create new ones. It allows us to reinvent ourselves and change our outcomes by changing how we think. This means that no matter what age you are and what stage of life you are in, the opportunity for change is limitless as long as you are willing to take the first step.

Real change is not mammoth or all-encompassing. Rather it is the small deliberate actions that we take each day that pave the way for real change. New habits have the power to give us a new lease on life. Every time you want to turn a new page in the story of your life, start by making routine changes that will become milestones on the journey to accomplishing your goal.

In your journey to becoming mentally strong and resilient, invest yourself in the process and the results will be inevitable. Commit to doing something out of your comfort zone each day and you will find that you are no longer bound by fear or lack of determination. Remember your best weapon against indecision, procrastination, and fear is action. The minute you take the first step, you are already halfway there.

You have already taken the first step to building your mental strength and toughness by reading this book. The next step is to use the strategies you have learned in this book to gradually become more resilient and committed to your dreams. Remember you do not have to do it all at once. Start small by looking at the things that hold you back the most and build yourself from there.

The lessons in this book are meant to give you a new lease of life and open your eyes up to all the opportunities that you miss when you get into the habit of quitting. Start using the strategies and tools you have learned to empower yourself to become mentally tough and resilient. We hope that the information you have learned in this book will help you achieve your goals and realize your dreams!

BOOK 2
Procrastination:
Shut Up and Do Those Damn Things!

An Ass-Kicking Guide to Stop Procrastinating, Cure Laziness, and Destroy Bad Habits. Your Productivity Action Plan for
UNLIMITED SUCCESS

Introduction

How can you do the things you really need to be doing if you have gotten so damn good at finding other things to do instead? Contrary to popular belief procrastination is really not about laziness. Of course, you can be both a procrastinator and lazy, but more often than not procrastination is an emotional resistance issue.

If you stop to think about it, you will realize that when you procrastinate you still somehow manage to find the energy and time to do less important stuff. So even as you are saying, *I just don't have time to do this now*, what you really mean is, *I would rather do something else with my time.* In essence, procrastination is usually a way to avoid doing things that challenge our feelings, our beliefs, the way we think of ourselves, and even our view of the world.

If you have perfected the art of the last-minute, or you are always finding yourself on the wrong side of the clock, then you probably realize that procrastination is not just a quirk. This self-defeating habit can impact your productivity and seriously diminish your ability to seize opportunities and achieve your goals. In fact, as far as self-sabotage goes, procrastination is one of the easiest ways to do it.

Like any other habit, procrastination develops over time as a coping mechanism to help us deal with negative emotions. The good news is that since it is a habit, you have the power to break it and go from being a sit-on-your-ass kind of person to getting-shit-done.

This book, *Stop Procrastination*, is meant for anyone tired of feeling like a deer caught in the headlights every time they need to make a decision. If you want to overcome the inaction that is caused by fear and become more proactive, this book will empower you to do just that. We take a brutally honest look at why people procrastinate and give you in-depth insights as to why you find it easy to put off important tasks or decisions.

We will provide an in-depth look at the emotional nature of procrastination and why this habit can have a strong hold over your life and outcomes. If you have been wondering why you simply seem to have no control over the direction your life is going in, you will find useful insights in this section of the book.

The bulk of this practical guide is dedicated to practical tools and strategies that you can use every day to beat procrastination. We aim to empower you to become more proactive and help you get things done without waiting for the "perfect" moment or just the "right" opportunity. If you are tired of watching things happen, this is the guide you have been waiting for to help you get your shit together, no pun intended.

Chapter 1: The Art of Playing Catch Up

How do you know what moment caused the car crash? Is there a tipping point that marked the moment when your career started to take a nosedive? Or even when your spouse decided they were done with you? The tricky thing about the big moments and the tipping points in your life is that you can only define them in retrospect. Sure, given some time and with the benefit of hindsight, you can probably see your past mistakes in excruciating clarity. But what about the ones you are making now, are they so obvious?

If only we could live life backward then we would know exactly where the pitfalls are and how to sidestep them. Unfortunately, that's not how it works. In the absence of a crystal ball to predict the future all you can do is make better choices today. Each day from the moment you wake up, your life is a series of choices. From what time you will wake up, what you do first thing, how you spend your day, and so on. Even when you are not consciously aware of it, you are constantly choosing.

The sum total of these choices is what determines where you are now and where you are likely to be in the future. This simply means that while you may not be able to see into the future, your actions today could probably give you a good indication of where you are apt to wind up. While this gives you power and control over your outcomes, the nature of these outcomes will depend on the kind of choices that you are making today.

The thing about making choices is that sometimes even when you know what the right choice is, you still make the wrong decision. Like when you have an exam or important work presentation tomorrow but going out with your friends is just more fun, or when you need to go to the gym but you choose to sleep in. The truth is, the right choice is not always the most pleasant, so more often than not you choose to do what feels good instead of what you should be doing.

Instant gratification is just one of the many reasons why people keep putting off things. Truth be told we put off things for plenty of reasons. However, no matter what reason causes you to procrastinate, the net result of putting things off is that you are always playing catch up.

You did not do what you should have done last week, last month or even yesterday, so your today becomes all about trying to make up for the lost time. Ultimately this becomes a continuous cycle and suddenly your productivity goes to hell, your goals are further than ever and you suddenly become the guy who is always a dollar short and a day late.

Procrastination is putting off tasks or decisions. It involves intentionally delaying working on something or making a difficult decision. Essentially when you procrastinate, you are simply postponing the inevitable because sooner or later you will have to do the thing you are putting off or deal with the consequences of putting it off.

We all procrastinate. We put off things when they are challenging, or when they are boring, or when we just don't feel like doing them. In fact, you may even tell yourself that you work best under pressure and that waiting until the last minute is not such a bad thing. And it wouldn't be, if it was just a one-time thing. The trouble with procrastination is that it rarely ever is a one-time thing.

What starts with you putting off one thing today, turns into you putting off two things tomorrow to make time for the thing you did not do today. This is why essentially procrastination is the art of playing catch up. No matter how trivial the decision seems in the moment, the truth is when you put off things you are losing time, and one way or another you will have to make up for this lost time.

Types of Procrastination

Procrastination essentially means the same thing no matter what lies behind it. It means that you put off doing things or intentionally delay taking action. However the why's behind procrastination vary because people avoid things for different reasons.

Behavioral procrastination

Let's say you sit down to work on an important assignment or work presentation. Two minutes after you start, you find yourself engrossed in funny cat videos on YouTube. Or you suddenly feel the need to go feed the dog. Or you decide to text your friend and ask them how their date was? Behavioral procrastination is when we put things off as an avoidance mechanism.

Humans by and large are emotional beings and we spend a lot of time and effort trying to feel good. Even the best of us succumb to moods, lack of motivation, and the allure of instant gratification. Many times, when you find yourself procrastinating, it has very little to do with laziness. However, it does have a lot to do with emotions. This emotional resistance to things that we find difficult, unpleasant, or just plain boring is what leads to behavioral procrastination.

The minute you start working on something challenging and maybe not so pleasant, your brain immediately switches to other more gratifying activities that you could do instead. This is why two minutes into your productive workday, you are checking out the price of hats on Amazon or what's new on Netflix. Behavioral procrastination is simply a type of avoidance mechanism. You have a challenging task at hand and you are anxious about it, so you look for ways to distract yourself so that you can feel better.

Most procrastinators do not realize just how much this kind of procrastination impacts their productivity. This is because just like any other avoidant behavior, it is easy to make excuses for your procrastination. From, *I am just waiting for inspiration to strike*, to *I work better under pressure* or *I will make time later*. Procrastinators have mastered the art of making excuses because they do not want to face the real reason for their avoidance.

Behavioral procrastination is self-sabotage at its best. The more you put things off the more stressful your life becomes. You feel guilty and ashamed because deep down you know exactly what it is that you need to be doing but you are choosing not to do it. This kind of guilt makes the task even more difficult to complete because, in addition to the anxiety, you are now full of self-doubt and questioning your abilities.

Behavioral procrastination can become so ingrained that it becomes a self-defeating cycle to nowhere. Most people assume that procrastinators are always just lounging about. This could not be further from the truth. Procrastinators are very good at keeping themselves busy with other tasks to avoid doing what they really need to be doing. This is when, for instance, you will go on a cleaning spree instead of working on that thesis you have been sitting on for months. Or when you spend hours in the office responding to emails instead of doing the really important things.

When you find yourself keeping yourself occupied with other things to avoid doing something difficult or challenging, this is classic behavioral procrastination. Psychologists attribute procrastination to an unwillingness to question our beliefs and our ideas of who we are.

Let's say that you took a math test and failed. The next time you have a Math test coming up, you may dread it a little. No one wants to think of themselves as a failure. However, instead of studying to increase your chances of passing, you may actually avoid studying because it makes you question how smart you are and makes you feel inadequate. When we have created an idea or identity in our minds of who we are, then, anything that questions this belief becomes a threat and something that we avoid either consciously or subconsciously.

People who wait till the last minute to do their projects may be driven by a need to avoid going through their work and finding errors in it. After all, if you do it last minute then you can always say you did your best given the time you had. Now if this was to happen once or maybe twice, it would be damaging on some level but not fatal. However behavioral procrastination is just that, a behavior. It does not happen once or twice; procrastination more often than not morphs into a habit.

When you are a procrastinator you will often give in to the need for instant gratification. Wanting to feel good is a natural human instinct but it becomes a problem when it diverts your focus from your goals. When you cannot override your emotional impulses and stick with what you need to be doing chances are you keep putting off doing things. Even though you know that your actions today will impact your future, you are more likely to go with your emotional brain. The emotional brain is what tells you, *sleep one more hour,* or *why go to the gym when you can just stay home and chill,* or *work on that presentation tomorrow.*

When you do not feel connected to your future self, it is easy to make decisions based solely on what is good for you today. When you are not invested enough in your long-term goals to overcome the emotional resistance, you will always find that you struggle with staying focused. Ultimately behavioral procrastination is all about wanting to feel good and putting off things that challenge you or make you uncomfortable in any way. Remember it is not enough to know what you should be doing if you lack the self-discipline to follow through on it.

Decisional Procrastination

John has been offered the job of his dreams by a competing law firm. He is a junior partner at his current job and is pretty sure that's as far as he will go for the foreseeable future. The competitor is offering him a senior partnership position and all the perks that come along with it. Yet, he has been "considering" this offer for about a month and just cannot bring himself to jump ship. In many ways, he knows that it is the opportunity of a lifetime so why is it so hard to make a decision that could potentially change his life?

Every now and then you are faced with potentially life-changing decisions. It could be a career move, marrying your soulmate, picking your major in school, or anything else that could influence the rest of your life. Some people are sure of themselves and sure of what they want, so when faced with such decisions they do not hesitate. These are the guys who drop out of college to start a business or move to a different state to start all over again. Their confidence in themselves and passion for their goals gives them all the strength they need to get past their misgivings and go after what they want.

But what if you are on the other end of the spectrum? What if uncertainty scares you so much that you would rather stay where you are than take a chance on something new. Decisional procrastination is when you are unable to make important decisions because you are afraid of uncertainty. You prefer to exist within your comfort zone so you rarely go after opportunities that require you to push yourself or change in any way. Decisional procrastination is characterized by inaction and freezing in the big moments.

The markets are too unpredictable, the new job will mean a longer commute, if I leave I may never find someone again.... All these are excuses that give you permission to stay where you are. These excuses are really just fear masquerading as logic. Decisional procrastination is so damaging because it makes you blind to opportunities. It makes you incapable of stepping up and showing up when the moments call for it. You are always afraid of what may happen or of failing. You see the opportunity but it requires you to leave your comfort zone so you end up doing nothing at all.

People who are prone to decisional procrastination all have one thing in common. They often feel stuck in one way or another but they never do anything to change their situation. They will complain about their jobs, their spouses, their finances, and everything else under the sun. What they will not do is take a chance on something new. Decisional procrastination leads to inaction or paralysis which means that making any progress in your life becomes almost impossible.

Perfectionists for instance suffer from decisional procrastination. They will obsess over every little detail and wait until everything is "just right" to do something. Of course, since things rarely if ever become "just right" perfectionists are classic procrastinators. They plan and plan but rarely do these plans see the light of day because there is always something amiss.

If you are constantly afraid of the possibility of failure, then chances are you always put off important decisions. You may find it difficult to seize opportunities even when they are staring you right in the face. This is because you often let your fear of failure overpower your need to go after your goals. Decisional procrastination is so paralyzing because it hides a fear of uncertainty and an unwillingness to step outside of your comfort zone.

Just like behavioral procrastination, decisional procrastination is also self-sabotage at its finest. When you are prone to inaction due to indecision, you do not need any other enemies. This is because you are the biggest stumbling block to your own progress. Unless you can find a way to beat decisional procrastination, you will always find that your dreams are always so near yet somehow still out of reach.

The Stages of Procrastination
a) Self-delusion

I have plenty of time to get this done, If I move some things around tomorrow, I will have time to work on this, the deadline *is still far...*These are the kinds of things that you tell yourself when you want to avoid doing something. You give yourself a false sense of security. You assume that tomorrow you will be in a better mood, or it will be easier or you will magically figure out how to do it.

Tomorrow is always the lifeline you use when you know very well that it should be done today. This is the first stage of procrastination. Making excuses and permitting yourself to not do what needs to be done.

b) *Laziness*

Plain old laziness or simply not wanting to inconvenience yourself is the second stage of procrastination. Sometimes you simply do not want to put in the effort required to get something done so of course, the easiest thing to do is to put it off to some other time. I will study for the exam tomorrow. *I will apply for the job next week, I will go to the gym on Monday, I will study for the exam next week, I will figure it out tomorrow...*there are endless excuses that we use to avoid doing something when the effort feels like its too much trouble.

Laziness is not just physical but it is actually connected to how your brain works. If a particular event does not carry enough of a reward to motivate you, you will always find yourself unwilling to put in the effort. In much the same way that a reward motivates you to get off your ass, if the reward is not sufficient, you will not be inspired to act. Think of how exhausted you feel when working on some work project but the minute your friend calls and asks you to go out for drinks you perk right up and the exhaustion mysteriously disappears.

When an activity carries a bigger emotional reward, it is no surprise that you will find it much easier to do than something that has no immediate emotional payoff. That is why one task can feel so exhausting even when you are barely using any physical effort while another feels so exhilarating.

Most people will prioritize pleasure over their work because pleasure feels good. When you are doing something you enjoy, like playing a video game, the emotional reward is instant. You are having fun so the reward is immediate. In contrast, when you are studying for a test, the reward is something far off in the future. This means the thought of passing your exam may be less of a motivator because it is not an immediate reward.

c) Manipulation and denial

Procrastinators are masters of manipulation. They pass off their inability to do what is required as someone else's fault or unavoidable circumstances. They will often say things like, *I have too much on my plate*, *if I was not under so much pressure I would have,* or *the timing was just bad...* and similar excuses. Since you do not want to admit to yourself that you are intentionally delaying doing something then you will start to look for scapegoats.

At this stage of procrastination, you have realized that you have boxed yourself into a corner. However, instead of admitting your fault, you find it easier to play the victim by finding excuses to explain why you did not do what you were supposed to. For most people denial is a way to avoid facing the fact that they are responsible for whatever mess they created.

It is so much easier to look in the mirror when you can blame your boss, your spouse, the weather, and everything in between. Think of excuses such as, *there is no point in applying for the promotion, my boss doesn't like me anyway*. Or, *I just do not have time to do a good job on this so I would rather not do it*. In both of these examples, you have given yourself permission to not try. You have explained away your inability to do what you need to so you do not have to feel like you have let yourself down.

The reason denial is so damaging is that it gives us blind spots. When you cannot see your own mistakes or the ways in which you self-sabotage, the probability that you will beat procrastination is pretty low. Self-awareness is a crucial part of understanding your habits and without this awareness, you will always feel like you are swimming against the current.

What is Procrastination Costing You
You know that sinking feeling you get when you know you are about to screw up (*again*)? That disappointment you feel when you see something that was within reach slip between your fingers because you did not do what you were supposed to? The moment when you know that you dropped the ball and it is too late to undo it? The consequences of procrastination are always more costly for you than they are for others.

When you habitually procrastinate you will often let other people down. But most of all you will always let yourself down. You will often find yourself feeling inadequate or even incompetent. You will question your ability, your work ethic, and most of all your self-esteem will plummet. This internal cost of procrastination just makes it even more difficult for you to beat your inner fears and hesitation. Without confidence taking action is always going to be difficult so procrastination almost always becomes a self-defeating cycle.

As a procrastinator, your personal relationships suffer because you are always unreliable and people can never really count on you. People get used to you always disappointing them in one way or another. You are always late, you miss important events because, no surprise, you are always short on time. You find that most people in your life think that you are lazy or indifferent. This of course means that you are constantly at odds with the people in your life.

Procrastination is especially damaging when it comes to productivity. When you cannot manage your time well and prioritize important tasks then your performance is likely to be average at best if not downright mediocre. Your colleagues may think you are the office slacker and your boss probably does not take you too seriously. Most procrastinators will find that their careers stall and they seem to be stuck in the same positions year in year out. This has more to do with their inability to step up when required to and very little to do with a lack of skills.

As a procrastinator, you probably miss more opportunities than you seize. You are always talking or thinking about going after your goals but when it comes to execution you balk. You are probably the type of person who has had a brilliant business idea for years but is yet to do anything about it. You want to step up in your career but you never go for promotions when the opportunity arises or apply for new jobs. In essence, procrastination is one of the most damaging types of self-sabotage. Unfortunately, you never really realize this until it is too late.

Often you may think, *what is the harm in doing this next week or tomorrow*? In the moment delaying something may seem trivial or inconsequential but the impact that procrastination has on your productivity tends to gather momentum as time passes. The more last-minute things that you have to do because you put them off, the higher your stress levels are. Procrastination is not just self-sabotage but it also increases significantly the amount of stress that you have to deal with every day.

Playing catch up means that you are never quite at ease. You always have something that you need to compensate for or make excuses for. Your friends do not trust you because you are the person who always shows up late, backs out of plans last-minute, and rarely does what they say they will. Procrastination affects how others see you and it also affects how you see yourself.

When you can never really be sure that you will be able to get things done, your confidence is undermined. You approach challenges with self-doubt and fear because you know that there is a high chance that you will either accomplish the task late or fail to finish. Ultimately procrastination is the gap between intent and action. When you put things off you are aware of what you should be doing, you are probably aware of the consequences of putting it off, and yet, you still cannot bring yourself to do it.

If you are walking down the street and there is a huge gaping hole in the ground, naturally you will walk around it. Nobody will knowingly walk into a pitfall that they can see because your natural instinct for self-preservation kicks in. However, mental pitfalls are not that easy to sidestep. When you procrastinate, you know what you should be doing but you cannot bring yourself to do it. This means that you are constantly walking into pitfalls not because you cannot see them but because you do not know how to stop yourself.

Ultimately procrastination has external and internal costs. It will impact your success on a variety of fronts including finances, career, productivity relationships, and personal growth. In terms of the internal cost that procrastination has on your life, you will experience constant stress, low self-esteem, shame, guilt, and worst of all regret.

Are you a Procrastinator?
One of the stages of procrastination is denial and naturally like many of our blind spots we rarely look in the mirror for a solution. So, if you find yourself not quite sure whether you are in the habit of procrastination, here are some characteristics of procrastination that you need to be on the lookout for.

I. You are always late. You turn in your work late; you show up late for meetings and are rarely ever on time.
II. You are constantly frazzled. You are always trying to beat the clock because well, you are late.
III. You often experience panic and stress over an uncompleted task that is due or sometimes overdue. You feel that you are constantly under pressure and never quite prepared for whatever is coming.
IV. You rarely have a schedule or a deliberate plan of action to accomplish tasks. You specialize in "winging it" and mostly wait to get into the right mood to start doing something.
V. You have plenty of half-completed tasks on your desk that you keep meaning to finish but never quite get around to doing.

VI. You are always complaining about how busy you are but have very little to show for it at the end of the day.
VII. You are easily distracted and you find yourself constantly switching from one task to another without really focusing on anything in particular.
VIII. Your workspace is constantly cluttered and you often misplace things or forget where you left an important document and file.
IX. You have a lot on your mind and you often feel overwhelmed.
X. When tackling your to-do list, you almost always start with the easy things and put off anything difficult or challenging.

Most people procrastinate to some degree. The real damage is when procrastination becomes a way of life. If you answered yes to most of the above questions, you are a procrastinator and this habit may be costing you a lot more than you think.

Chapter 2: Why do You Procrastinate

In Greek mythology, Odysseus the hero of the Trojan war almost succumbed to the enchantment of the devious Sirens. Even forewarned, Odysseus still found himself struggling to ignore the enchanting song of the Sirens. These mythical creatures had been the downfall of many men and their Island was littered with the bones of the hapless men who had succumbed to their baser instincts and heeded the call of the Sirens.

In this mythical tale, Odysseus is no ordinary man; in fact, he has just won the Trojan war. However, his journey back home is not a sure shot. The goddess Circe warns him of the Sirens, demons in disguise who lure men to their death with their enchanting songs. Wise man that he is, Odysseus fills his comrades' ears with bee wax to keep them safe from the charms of the Sirens. However, he decides that he wants to hear the enchanting Siren song and survive so he does not put wax in his ears.

As they sail across the ocean, the draw of the Sirens' song is so strong that Odysseus is only saved from sure death by his comrades. In this mythical tale, it is not the war in itself that threatens to befall Odysseus, in fact, he is on his way home a hero. The real danger to this hero is the distraction of the Sirens who are the true test of his will.

You may not be a Greek hero or a hero of any type for that matter, but just like Odysseus, your inner enemy is far more dangerous than any external enemy you will ever need to face. The short story is, half of the battles you lose, you lose them on the inside long before you ever lose them on the outside.

But what does all this have to do with procrastination you may be wondering? Indeed, what exactly is procrastination? Simply put procrastination is intentionally delaying doing something or putting off for tomorrow what you need to do today. In essence, procrastination involves going against your better judgment and willfully avoiding certain tasks or responsibilities.

It is easy to get it twisted and confuse procrastination with laziness. It is not that simple. Of course, there is definitely an aspect of laziness in procrastination. After all, you are not putting off taking out the garbage or working on your assignment because you are in mortal peril. You just do not want to get off your ass, because, well let's face it watching Netflix is much more pleasurable. However, there is so much more to habitual procrastination than laziness.

Have you been stuck in the same miserable dead-end job for years because you just cannot bring yourself to apply for the job that you know is great for you? Are you two years down a toxic relationship but just cannot get up the will to leave even when you know it will end in tears? Have you been planning to open your dream business for the past five years? Are you dreading that test next week because you know that you have not studied for it?

Whatever it is that you are choosing *NOT* to do against your better judgment, there is no doubt that procrastination is one of the biggest stumbling blocks to achieving your goals and turning your life around. So why do we procrastinate? Why is it so easy to think *I'll do it tomorrow?* To really understand why you procrastinate. We must first demystify the different types of procrastinators.

The Perfectionist

The perfectionist is perhaps more susceptible to procrastination than any other personality type. If you are a perfectionist, you spend more time obsessing over every little detail and of course the more caught up you are in the details, the less time you spend actually getting things done.

For the perfectionist, it's never quite the "right" time start. They are always waiting for everything to fall into place so they can make their move. The perfectionist needs all their ducks to be neatly lined up in a row so that they can take the shot. Unfortunately, this is life, and things are rarely if ever perfect. So, what happens is that the perfectionist misses opportunity after opportunity because the conditions are never just right enough for them to get going or get started on whatever they need to do.

Have you missed a deadline at work because you were obsessing over the small details of your presentation? Have you lost the girl of your dreams because you were waiting for the "right" time to ask her out only for a Johnny-come-lately to beat you to the punch and sweep her off her feet? Perfectionists do not just miss out on opportunities; their productivity is often impaired and they are always on the wrong side of the clock. While you are busy planning and waiting for the right time, life is passing you by because unfortunately, time stops for no one.

If you are a perfectionist, then you are probably full of brilliant ideas that never quite see the light of day. You spend hours and hours planning and preparing but never actually on the execution of those plans. The trouble with perfection is that it is a fallacy, the more you chase it the more elusive it becomes. If you are constantly trying to get everything just right then you probably get less done than someone who may be less skilled or talented but subscribes to the *Just do It* motto.

Each one of us has a desire to get things right, however, for the perfectionist, their fear of getting anything wrong far outweighs the need to get things done. This fear of failure is the root cause of procrastination. The fear of failure makes many people not try at all because they would rather not try at all than fail. Since cavemen were running from predators, fear has always been and is still one of the biggest motivators known to man. Unfortunately, fear can either motivate you into action or inaction.

Like a deer in the headlights, a perfectionist is always too scared to move forward. Their fear of failure paralyzes them into inaction so instead of doing what needs to be done, they find a hundred and one reasons not to do it. *I would have asked for the raise if my boss if the deal had closed, I do not have all the capital I need to start, I will ask her out tomorrow when there is a full moon out, I will write the book when I feel inspired....*

A perfectionist will find excuses not to act and these excuses range from the mundane to plain delusional. The end result is a lot of missed opportunities and dreams that never quite make it to real life. For a perfectionist, it is all about the small stuff, they sweat it and they make it bigger than the bigger picture. All the while not knowing that it is the fear of failure that is holding them back.

If you are too busy obsessing over the small details, chances are you have been putting off doing what you need to do because you are waiting for some "magical" perfect moment that will never come. You miss out on potentially life-changing opportunities because you are too afraid to make a mistake or fail. If this is you, the only thing you will perfect over time is the art of self-sabotage because ultimately you are the biggest stumbling block in your path.

The Dreamer

Dreams are great when you are asleep, but not so much if they take up your waking hours as well. Dreamers are legendary procrastinators. They are always so lost in an alternate reality that they forget to actually live in the moment. A dreamer is similar to a perfectionist because they are always full of plans and ideas but never really get around to executing them.

This is the guy who has been planning to open a business for the past seven years or the one who is always talking about going back to school but never really doing anything about it. Dreamers are great when it comes to ideas and plans but not so great with execution. They have plenty of things they want to accomplish but never really have a solid plan or goal they are working towards.

Dreamers procrastinate because they have an aimless approach to life. If you always know what you want but have no real structure or plan on how to get it, then you are most probably a dreamer. You have no problem coming up with brilliant ideas, it is the how-to that seems to elude you. The trouble with being a dreamer is that your brilliance rarely does you any good because you seldom get around to actually doing anything with it.

The notion that you can just float around in life and things will somehow just come your way is a great hindrance to productivity. If you do not have an actual purpose or goal in mind then you will always have trouble making decisions and being proactive. How can you choose which path to take if you have no real destination in mind?

For dreamers, their procrastination is caused by a lack of purpose or effective goal setting. If you are a dreamer you are probably prone to making vague declarations like, *I want to lose weight, or I need a better job, or my love life sucks.* While you may have the right intentions, your goal has no real power over you because it is not specific or time-bound. Consider the difference between saying, *I want to lose 10 pounds by the end of this month* versus saying *I want to lose weight.*

In one scenario you have set yourself a clear and measurable goal that has a timeline. In the other scenario, you do not have a specific goal or time frame in mind but rather a wistful thought. Naturally, you are more likely to be more motivated in the first scenario because you know not just what you want, but when you want it.

The dreamer lacks the motivation to do what needs to be done because they traffic in wishes, not goals. The difference between a wish and a goal is that a goal is something you work towards while a wish is something you want to be granted. Every day the dreamer will have a new idea to replace the old one and no clue as to how to bring that idea to life.

For the dreamer, the real challenge is in snapping out of their slumber and actually working towards something tangible. Dreamers procrastinate not because they do not know what they want but rather because they are not motivated enough to get up and go after what they want.

The Octopus
If you are the type of person who is always working on ten different projects at a time, then you are no stranger to putting things off. A Multi-tasker or an octopus procrastinator is a person who tries to do so much at once that they end up never getting anything done.

If you are this type of procrastinator then your desk is probably littered with half-finished projects and things that you simply forgot about.

Contrary to popular opinion multi-tasking does not make you more productive. Research has actually shown that multitasking reduces your brain's efficiency. This means that when you are trying to do so many tasks at once, you do them less efficiently than you would if you tackled one task at a time.

Unfortunately, we live in a high-pressure world where at any given time you are trying to juggle many different things. This is what has bred a society of people who are always fraught, exhausted, and operating on nothing but fumes. If you are constantly juggling multiple tasks, taking on more than you can handle, and trying to manage everything at once, chances are you are mentally exhausted. This mental exhaustion impairs productivity and keeps you from doing what you really need to be doing.

If you find that you always have a pile of half-finished projects, or that you are always busy but nothing is getting done, its time to re-evaluate your approach. It is important to remember that busyness and productivity are not the same thing. Is your work yielding results or are you simply wearing yourself out on a treadmill of never-ending work and responsibilities? When you are constantly multi-tasking it is easy to get your priorities upside down and neglect to do the things that really matter.

When you have an octopus mentality, you have trouble delegating or saying no to tasks. This means that instead of concentrating on one task and doing it well, you always end up with a bunch of things to do that end up wasting your time and taking your attention away from more important issues. Most people with this kind of mentality are afraid that if they do not keep all their balls spinning then they will have failed in some way.

For instance, you will find women or even men who are struggling to juggle work and parenthood successfully because they do not want to give up on either. They want to prove themselves at work yet still be there for their children so they end up running themselves ragged on both ends. The net result is that they underperform on both ends and start to get disillusioned with life.

Knowing how to prioritize your responsibilities, recognizing when your plate is full and most importantly knowing when you need help can be one of the most empowering things you can do for yourself. People who get things done understand their limits and do not try to take on the whole world themselves. Remember to be productive, you actually have to finish what you start so it is more important to stick with a few projects that you can do well than run yourself ragged on twenty different things you will probably never finish.

The Pleasure Seeker
If instant gratification was a drug, there would be a whole lot of people hooked on it. A lot of procrastination comes down to people choosing to do that which is more pleasurable and avoiding unpleasant tasks or decisions. We all to some degree fall into this category where we put off things that we consider difficult or hard for later because we would rather do something more pleasurable. This kind of avoidance can quickly become a habit and affect your productivity.

Think of the simple choices that you make every day. Seemingly mundane choices like choosing to watch your favorite show instead of going to the gym or spending your time chatting on social media instead of working on a project are all little ways in which we prioritize pleasure over pain or hard work. The problem with instant gratification is that it develops into a habit and before you know it, you have little self-discipline to keep you on track.

When the pursuit of instant gratification becomes an ingrained habit, every difficult or unpleasant task will be relegated to the back burner. This means that your life will start to revolve around pleasure and you will lose sight of what you stand to gain by prioritizing what is important over what is pleasurable. Addictions, for instance, are borne out of an inability to resist momentary pleasure no matter how damaging it is in the long run.

The science behind the need for instant gratification is explained by the fact that the brain is hardwired to follow the path of least resistance. Your brain will always choose the easy way out because there is no emotional resistance to doing pleasurable things. For instance, between studying for an exam or going out parting with your friends, the easy choice is going out because it is more pleasurable.

The problem with seeking instant gratification is that the more you do it the more habitual it becomes. Think of how many times a downward spiral in your life was set off by a seemingly innocuous decision that you made. One day you woke up and you decided to skip the gym that day because you were tired. The next day you decided you would go later in the day. Before you knew it, two months had passed without going to the gym and you were twenty pounds overweight.

When we procrastinate, the consequences may not be evident in the present but gradually the impact on productivity becomes inevitable. Let's say you are in college. If you skip a class this week, no big deal, if you skip two next week, again no big deal. However, if in a month you start to skip whole weeks at a time then the shit really hits the fan. Your grades will start to go down the drain and you will barely be able to keep up in class.

Whether you are aware of it not, every choice you make sets off a chain reaction that can quickly take you from *no big deal* to *what the hell happened?* Instant gratification is like slapping a band-aid on something and hoping it goes away. You will indulge yourself in the present but reality is always waiting to slap you in the face on the other side.

Let's take an example of Mark for example. He has an important meeting with new clients at the office. Instead of preparing for this crucial meeting, he gets distracted chatting with his friends on social media. He barely gets any work done and this is evident in the meeting where he stumbles through a shoddy presentation. If this happens once, Mark may get away with it and his boss will probably think he is having an off day.

But what if it happens time and time again? At best he will be considered a slacker and his career will stagnate, or at worst he may end up losing his job. Now if Mark was to go back in time to the point where he chose the more fun activity, instead of his work it probably did not feel like a big deal. However, a small deal can quickly turn into a shit show if you are not careful. It is the little decisions that you make daily that have the biggest impact on your life. It is pretty easy to choose pleasure over pain, but are you ready for the consequences?

The Goldfish
Are you easily distracted? Do you often find yourself fleeting from one thing to the next? People who have a short attention span end

up putting off important things not because they are lazy or scared of failure but simply because they have the attention span of a goldfish.

This is the type of procrastinator who will start working on one thing, notice something else that is seemingly more interesting, and as a result abandon the first task. As a result, this type of procrastinator never really finishes anything they start because they are so easily distracted. The allure of the new, and simple curiosity can quickly turn you into someone who is always putting off things that need to be done because you are too distracted to do them.

For some people, the distraction can be your co-workers, your friends, or even your hobbies. When you cannot focus long enough on a task to finish it then inevitably, you will always find yourself rushing to beat the clock or constantly failing to get things done. The productivity of someone who is easily distracted is pretty low since they have little self-control. This means that for people with a short attention span the only way to beat procrastination is to consciously manage their work environment in such a way that it is free of distractions.

If you find yourself checking your phone every two minutes, maybe its time to switch it off and focus on your work or whatever you need to get done. If your co-workers are distracting you from an important project, find a quiet space to work in. The bottom line is that you need to have enough self-awareness to understand the kinds of distractions that stop you from getting things done and get in the way of you reaching your goals.

When it comes to procrastination, the biggest problem is the little choices that we make every day. Do not be fooled into thinking that procrastination only becomes an issue when it comes to life-changing decisions. It starts with the mundane, then slowly becomes a habit that is holding you hostage, and eventually, you find that you are no longer in control of your outcomes, your goals are further than ever and you have no idea how you got here.

Chapter 3: The Overthinking Trap

A disenchanted teenager depressed by the inadequacy of his own life compared to what he sees on Instagram. The disillusioned employee who is certain her boss is out to get her because he ignored her in the meeting. The hypochondriac who thinks they are dying of everything because the symptoms on google hit close to home. The wife who thinks her husband is having an affair because he did not notice the new haircut. It is a small wonder that there are still any sane people left in the world.

Thinking is what sets man apart from lesser beings. We are capable of thought and it is these thoughts that have led to civilization as we know it. But there is a difference between thinking and overthinking. Your thoughts tend to influence the way see yourself, the way you perceive others, and the way you interact with other people. Positive people are positive in nature for the simple reason that their thoughts are predominantly positive. Negative Nancy's on the other hand are negative because they are constantly thinking thoughts of gloom and doom.

When you are watching a sport on tv, usually there is a commentator giving a blow by blow account of the game. If the commentator gets excited, inevitably your anticipation increases. If the commentator is slow and not very enthusiastic chances are you will find the game boring. Your inner thoughts make up the inner voice. This inner voice is a commentator of sorts in your head that gives you a blow by blow account of your life. The more excited or enthused this inner voice is, the more confident and passionate you feel. The more negative or gloomy this inner commentator is, the more sluggish and uninspired you are likely to be.

Thoughts inevitably direct your actions and your behavior. Who you are is a product of the kind of thoughts you have. The link between overthinking and procrastination is unmistakable. The more you ruminate over events, over-analyze every single detail, and dissect every little word people say, the more likely you are to talk yourself out of doing something.

Overthinking differs from normal thinking in that it involves reading too much into situations. It is when you work yourself up into a frenzy over a situation or incident because you have let it become much bigger than it really is. When you overthink you most likely get caught up in worries for the future or regrets over the past. This means that overthinking rarely has anything to do with problem-solving. Most of the time when you overthink you are engaged in blaming, fault-finding, guilting, and worrying.

Most of the time you will find that overthinking is driven by negative emotions such as fear, loss, or anger. When, for instance, you are fretting over an exam or a big presentation, it is probably because you are focusing on all the ways you can mess it up. *What if my slides do not open, what if the client hates it, what if I miss the point entirely, what if they mock me, what if it's not good enough…?*

All these thoughts are not based on facts. You have no way of knowing how the presentation will go but you have chosen to focus on everything that might go wrong. This in a nutshell is what overthinking does. It chips away at your confidence, makes mountains out of molehills, and increases your susceptibility to procrastination.

Making Mountains Out of Molehills

How do you know when you have crossed the line from thinking to overthinking? Here are the most common signs that indicate that you are prone to overthinking.

- You relive your mistakes and embarrassing moments constantly
- Your thoughts are populated with lots of "what if" questions
- You over-analyze people's actions and words looking for a deeper meaning
- You worry about the future constantly and often find yourself absent-minded
- You often replay conversations in your head thinking of what you should have said or not said
- You spend a lot of time worrying about things that you cannot control

The one thing that sets apart overthinking from normal thinking is that it is rarely positive. You will hardly spend hours thinking about the client you just won but you are likely to think about it for days if you lose a client. Overthinking tends to lead to catastrophizing. This is when everything takes on epic doomsday proportions and you become obsessed with thoughts of failure.

It is no surprise that overthinking is one of the most common reasons why people procrastinate. It starts off with a seemingly mundane thought like, *I screwed up last time I had better be careful this time*. Then it progresses to, *why did they give me this assignment*, then, *I bet they are setting me up for failure*. Then this becomes, *I always knew he did not like me that's why I get all the hard tasks*. From this you go to, *I know I will lose my job if I fail this time*. Before long you are worrying about how you will be paying your mortgage without a job and whether your wife will leave you when you get fired.

This is the trajectory of overthinking. A simple incident turns into a catastrophe in a matter of minutes. All this of course is going on in your head and has no real basis in fact or your circumstances. Overthinking leads to procrastination because it puts you in a state where you are constantly anticipating the worst. In this state, it starts to make sense to delay doing something because in your mind by delaying you are also putting off the impending failure.

If you think back to the opportunities that you missed or the times that you did not step up, you will find that it was most likely due to overthinking. You talked yourself out of doing something because in your mind this thing took on larger than life proportions. A simple pitch became a career-defining moment, a date with your crush reminded you of how your first girlfriend dumped you, and so on. When you overthink, you tend to develop a natural talent for turning molehills into mountains. You are constantly looking for the nuance and hidden meaning behind what people say, and nothing is really just what it is.

Overthinking makes procrastination the easy way out because in your mind you are avoiding imminent disaster. People who overthink are in a constant state of anxiety and so it is no surprise that they become prone to inaction. When you engage in overthinking you are constantly feeding your fears and your self-doubt. This takes away your confidence and makes you a prisoner to your own negativity.

When you get into a habit of catastrophizing, you will often feel powerless and ill-equipped to take on whatever is happening in your life. This is because one of the most important weapons that you have in your arsenal is self-belief. When you magnify everything into an impossible task, your belief in your abilities shrinks. This makes it difficult to act and you become a perpetual procrastinator who puts things off because they are afraid of failing or falling short in some way.

Negative Self-Talk

Negative self-dialogue is something that a lot of people are not really aware of engaging in. You rarely stop to question your thoughts or your feelings. In fact, sometimes you may not even be aware of what you are thinking or even why you are feeling a certain way. Have you ever just caught yourself feeling under the weather for no apparent reason? Or have you had days when you just feel on top of the world?

Your moods can sometimes be a mystery. Unfortunately, this means that sometimes your thoughts and emotions will influence your behavior without you being consciously aware of it. Negative self-talk occurs when you keep having self-limiting thoughts and beliefs about yourself. When you are prone to negative self-talk, you are most likely your own worst critic. You are always focused on your weaknesses and barely even acknowledge your strengths.

Negative self-talk can take on the form of any of the following thinking traps.

Generalizations

I'll never get a new job, I am always late, he will never appreciate what I do, they never approve my projects, this always happens to me...do any of these thoughts sound familiar? If you are prone to generalizations you tend to make sweeping assumptions based on a single event or experience. You fail one Math test and, in your mind, you start to believe that you are no good at Math. Or you deliver a bad presentation and you start to think you are horrible at your job.

Generalizations are self-limiting because they put a cap on what you think you can do. When you attach a label to yourself based on a single experience you effectively deny yourself the opportunity to improve or to change. *I am a nerd* stops just being a thought and actually becomes who you are. The problem with generalizations is that they result in self-deception. You start to believe things about yourself that are simply not true.

The more you generalize, the smaller the box you have to operate within becomes. Your start to exist withing invisible walls that you have created for yourself that define what you can and cannot do. Obviously, generalizations will lead to procrastination. Every time you have to tackle something that goes beyond your beliefs of who you are and what you are capable of, you will find it difficult to start because you already have a preconceived notion about it.

For instance, if you believe that you never make effective pitches, chances are you will actively avoid any situation where you are required to pitch to a client. Since you already believe you will fail, you will not see the point in trying. Of course, if you do not try, your belief stays true because it is never proven otherwise. This is the self-defeating cycle of generalizations. It starts with a preconceived notion, that you reinforce over and over with your actions until it becomes your reality.

Minimization or magnification

Minimization is when you develop a tendency to magnify your flaws and overlook your strengths. This is when you have thoughts like, *why would they even consider me for the job, there are better candidates*. People who fall into this thinking trap are acutely aware of their weaknesses and yet oblivious of their strengths.

Minimization is characterized by being overly critical of yourself. With this kind of mindset, you regularly berate yourself for past mistakes and keep ruminating over every little thing you have done wrong. You find it easy to see where you went wrong but you seldom see any achievements that you have made.

Minimization is negativity at its best. It ensures that you are always focused on the negative and therefore have very little confidence or self-esteem to go on. The first thing you think when faced with a task is, *I bet I am going to screw this up* or *I am so stupid I will never figure this out*. These kinds of thoughts are not just limiting but emotionally damaging.

Negative thoughts inevitably lead to negative emotions and you become prone to chronic stress and anxiety. The most challenging thing about minimization is that you are hardly ever aware of it. These thoughts slowly creep up on you and before you know it all you can think about is what you did wrong.

Minimization often goes with magnification. This is where you habitually minimize your strengths and magnify your weaknesses. You take one failure to mean that you are doomed and every little mistake becomes a reason to berate yourself constantly.

The reason why this thinking trap is so debilitating is that you become your own worst enemy. Nobody needs to discourage you or bring you down because you are already doing a stellar job of it yourself. You hardly see anything good in yourself so there is no way you can communicate your value or worth to others. Any good salesman will tell you; it is pretty difficult to sell a product you do not believe in. If you do not believe in yourself then inevitably you will have trouble inspiring confidence and trust in others.

Assumptions

It is no surprise that people who overthink tend to make a lot of assumptions. They read too much into situations because they over-analyze every little detail. If you are prone to making assumptions then you are always focused on the hidden meaning, or reading between the lines. The trouble with assumptions is that sometimes they lead you to the wrong conclusions.

When you make decisions based on your assumptions, more often than not you get it wrong. Sometimes you can have an interaction with someone who is having a bad day. Even though they are being polite and responsive your mind starts to fixate on their coolness. You assume that they probably hate you or that you are doing or saying something wrong. Yet in actual sense, this person is dealing with things that really have nothing to do with you at all.

When you make assumptions, you do not just stop there. You use these assumptions to draw conclusions and then make decisions based on these conclusions. Ultimately you end up making the wrong decision because your assumption was off from the start. This thinking trap makes it difficult to assess situations and experiences objectively because for you there always has to be a hidden meaning and nothing is what it appears to be.

Black and white thinking

Black and white thinking is a common thinking trap that causes people to think in extremes. With this kind of thinking, you only have two possible outcomes in your mind. Black and white thinking is a common cause of procrastination because it leads you to think that things will with either go extremely well or extremely wrong.

If your thoughts only veer between the two extremes, you are either the best or you are nothing, you either excel or you fail or you either win or you lose. When you think in extremes even mundane tasks can become daunting and challenging. This is because you are unable to look at things from multiple perspectives. Instead of thinking, *this task is an opportunity for me to learn* you will approach it from the mindset that, *if I do not excel, I will be branded a failure* or *if I do not lose 10 pounds, I will be such a loser* and so on. Black and white thinking gives you a narrow point of view from which to operate and decreases your options.

Perfectionists often fall into this thinking trap because for them things need to be a certain way and if not, then it is unacceptable. With this kind of thinking, it becomes difficult to be enthusiastic about your work or other aspects of your life because you are always expecting either one of only two possible options. Win or lose.

Personalization

Personalization is a thinking trap where you take on responsibility for things that are beyond your control. This means that you take everything personally even when the circumstances have nothing to do with you. You are the kind of person who will think that people are out to get you or that you are just unlucky. You get offended easily and you always feel like everything is a test of your worth or value.

When your overthinking leads you to the personalization thinking trap, you will try to control circumstances and others because you feel like everything is about you. If you tend to feel like you need to fix everything, control everyone, and be responsible for everything then you probably have a tendency to overthink by personalizing everything.

Get Out of Your Head

Thinking is a good thing when you use it to come up with solutions to problems, make decisions, and to make plans. However, if your thinking is primarily made up of worries of the future or regrets of the past then you are not just thinking but overthinking. Overthinking takes your focus, energy, and time from the things you should be doing. It is a never-ending cycle because they will always be things to worry about and mistakes to ruminate over.

To beat procrastination, overthinking is one habit that you will have to ditch. This means getting out of your own head and becoming more present in the moment.

1) Learn to be more present

Being present means that you are acutely aware of what is going on in your life at that particular time. It means that you are connected and engaged in your life as it is happening. When you are constantly worrying about the future or the past, you become absent-minded and disconnected from your present. You let your fears of the future influence your decisions and you use your past mistakes to judge your present.

When you cultivate mindfulness, you learn to focus on the present. Your mind is not preoccupied with regrets of the past or worries about the future, this means that all the anxiety that stems from the fear of what will happen or your regrets over past mistakes no longer dominate your mind. People who procrastinate tend to do it because they are carrying emotional baggage that makes them apprehensive about the future.

When you are free of emotional baggage, you can approach each situation objectively. That is why learning to exist in the moment is one of the most effective ways to cultivate the mental strength that you need to overcome procrastination. Let the past be just that and strive to be connected and engaged with what is going on in your life in the present. Smell the roses, enjoy the process and stop being so caught up in worrying about the future.

Being present and mindful teaches you that if you do the right thing today, the future will take care of itself. Think of it this way, instead of obsessing about the 40 pounds that you need to lose, wouldn't it be much easier if you just focused on eating right today? When you get the steps and the process right, you never have to fear what the result is going to be.

Mindfulness helps you to overcome procrastination by equipping you with the confidence you need to take on whatever lies ahead. When you are present, you have control of what is happening to you because you are fully-engaged and living your life fully. If you are constantly absent-minded, stressed out, and just going through the motions, it's time to get out of your head and practice being more mindful.

People who overthink tend to be absent-minded because at any one point their mind is working a mile a minute. If you can learn to shut down the noise and keep your focus on what is going on around you, it will get easier to deal with whatever it is that you are facing. If your past and your future are not holding you back, then you have a lot less baggage to worry about and fret over.

Simple tips for mindfulness

I. Meditation is a great way to bring your thoughts back to the present, Simple meditation techniques can help you whenever you feel overwhelmed by thoughts or negative emotions.

II. Breathing exercises just like meditation are a great way to shut out the noise and bring your focus back to the present. Practice deep breathing before taking on a daunting task or making a difficult decision. This will help you calm down and give you the mental clarity that you need in such situations.

III. Staying active and healthy is not just good for your waistline. Physical exercises are a great way to deal with anxiety and boost your confidence. Even something as simple as taking a walk when you are mentally exhausted can help you to clear your mind and stay focused.

IV. There is something about writing things down that helps you to process your emotions and thoughts better. Journaling is a great way to stay connected to the present and avoid overthinking. It helps you process your feelings and build self-awareness. Make a habit of journaling to stay in touch with your inner self and create a healthy outlet for any negative thoughts and emotions.

V. Actively tune in to your thoughts. It is common for people to get so busy with life that they hardly pay attention to the kind of thoughts that are constantly running through their minds. Learn to listen to your thoughts and the kind of internal dialogue you are having with yourself.

2) Control the controllable

Traffic, weather, the economy, your boss's mood, your neighbor's opinion, all these things are external factors that you cannot control. Yet it is amazing how much time you spend worrying about them. When you are constantly weighed down by the things you cannot control, you lose precious time and energy that you could use on things that are actually within your control.

People who overthink tend to get into this habit because they obsess over every little detail. They worry about other people's opinions, they are scared of the competition, and they always think that if the circumstances were just right then everything would be okay. This is the kind of thinking that leads to procrastination because it makes you feel like there is never quite the right moment to act. You are waiting for your boss to start liking you before you ask for a raise, or you are waiting for the weather to get warmer so you can start jogging and so on.

To overcome procrastination, you must acknowledge that there will always be things that are outside of your control. You cannot control everything and that should not faze you because your outcomes are not defined by the circumstances. Your goals are dependent on you and your actions so focusing externally means you are just distracting yourself from what is actually important. It is pointless to worry and fret about things that you cannot control because worrying will not change anything.

Do not get overwhelmed by things that are not going to matter in a month or a year from now. To be truly dedicated to your goals you must be willing to let go of the distractions, that only cause you anxiety and stress. Life is always easier if you travel light so only take with you what you are going to use in the future. Everything else is unnecessary baggage.

Take the emotion out of it

Do you spend a lot of time waiting for inspiration to strike? Or, for the right mood so you can get started on what you need to do? There is no running away from emotions because the emotional brain is almost always stronger than our logical brain. We gravitate towards things that feel good because it is human nature to seek comfort and security. So how do you get past the emotional resistance that causes you to constantly avoid things that are uncomfortable and challenging?

Mentally strong people find a way to get past their emotions by cultivating discipline. They create deliberate plans and schedules that require them to do certain things at certain times in order to stay focused on their goals. The truth is their days when you will be absolutely out of it and feeling like all you want is to do nothing at all. A schedule or timetable helps you get past the low points because it leaves you with little room for emotion.

Something as simple as leaving you workout gear each night so that it is the first thing you see in the morning, or clearing any junk food out of your fridge will help you do the right thing regardless of how you are feeling. Motivation and inspiration are great to have but even more important is the self-discipline that will help you stay consistent. It doesn't matter how hard you work today if you are just going to slack off tomorrow. Consistency is what keeps you moving towards your goals.

Invest in processes and action plans that help you to stay committed and consistent in the pursuit of your goals. The more discipline you cultivate, the easier it will be to cultivate habits that are not influenced by your emotions. Gradually as you get into the habit of planning and scheduling you will find that you are no longer a prisoner to your emotions and moods.

Developing a Bias Towards Action

The human brain is wired to take the path of least the resistance. What this means is that naturally, we gravitate towards safety and comfort. If you have often wondered why you tend to follow routines and patterns of behavior it is simply because your brain is designed to take the safest and most familiar pathway. This is part of the self-preservation mechanism that the mind uses to keep us safe from risks and danger.

Procrastination is a common result of an inability to break away from your comfort zone and embrace uncertainty. When you are too afraid to take a chance or try something new, you become prone to indecision and inaction. This means you waste a lot of time thinking instead of getting things done. You become risk-averse and find it difficult to make decisions because you struggle with anything that does not feel familiar or comfortable.

Research has found that developing a bias towards action helps to overcome procrastination. It helps you worry less and do more. Having a bias towards action means you move from overthinking everything to embracing the *Just Do it* credo. Fortunately, anyone can develop a bias towards action and become more decisive and focused.

Tips for developing a bias towards action

- Stop multitasking

Contrary to popular opinion multi-tasking does not increase productivity. Studies have found that multitasking actually decreases brain efficiency. This means that the more you try to do, the less efficient you are. When you overwhelm yourself with distractions, multiple projects, and responsibilities, making decisions becomes hard. You become incapable of staying focused because your mind and your life are cluttered.

Learn to prioritize and organize your day in such a way that you are not trying to do everything all at once. Keep distractions to a minimum and avoid keeping things like social media on full time. When you are focused on a particular task, you get better mental clarity, and making decisions is not as daunting.

Learn to say no when your plate is full and always know which tasks are important in terms of reaching your goals. Always keep in mind that being busy and being productive are not always the same thing. Figure out what tasks should be top of your list and which ones come second. Conserving your energy for the important stuff makes you more efficient, more productive and a whole less stressed out.

- Baby steps

If have to get past a challenge or particularly difficult task, most of your fear comes from thinking about all the work that needs to be done. If you are writing a book and you keep thinking *how will I ever write 400 pages?* You will be overwhelmed by the sheer magnitude of what lies ahead of you. Or, if you want to lose weight and you keep thinking, *I need to lose 50 pounds*, this thought will make the task seem almost impossible.

If you tend to procrastinate because the task ahead of you seems too big, try breaking it down into smaller milestones. What can you do today to get to where need to go? Do not think of the whole 50 pounds you have to lose but rather focus on what you can do today to get started. When you break your goal down into bite-sized milestones, it becomes easier to get started and stay focused.

If you want to write start with the first page, then the first chapter, and the rest will follow. The hardest part especially for procrastinators is the first step. Once you get that out of the way, then following through on your goals will not be so daunting. Take your goal one day at a time and focus on the present. If you invest in the process, then the result will take care of itself.

- Create a system

To develop a bias towards action you have to create habits that push you towards your goals. This means creating a system that pushes you towards action. It can be as simple as leaving your work out gear each night so that it's the first thing you see when you wake up in the morning. Or making sure that you work on everything in your in-tray each day before you leave the office.

Systems make it easy to stick to the plan because they push you towards action. Do not leave your goals up to moods or emotions. Take deliberate steps towards your goal using a system that helps you stay committed and focused.

- The five-second rule

Sometimes the simplest way to get started is to just count down from 5 then start. This rule works because it stops you from overthinking. Most of the time when you hesitate it is because you are overthinking the situation. You are probably going through the *what-ifs, the shoulds, the shouldn'ts, the coulds*... and everything in between. Counting down to five stops the overthinking and prompts you to just get started and figure it out as you go.

Chapter 4: How Lazy Are You?

Procrastination may be laziness in disguise but laziness is not procrastination. It is easy to assume that procrastination and laziness are the same thing but this is not necessarily accurate. In some cases, you may procrastinate because you are not motivated enough to do the task. This, however, is different from not doing something because it is inconvenient or requires too much effort. Laziness is an unwillingness to put in the effort to get something done. It has nothing to do with fear of failure or self-doubt which are the main causes of procrastination.

When you do not want to do your homework, or when you dump your work on someone else at work, this is just laziness. It has nothing to do with procrastination. Laziness is usually an indication that you lack the intrinsic motivation required to get up and do something. You either feel that the task is too much work, or that it is not worth the effort.

Laziness stems from either a lack of interest in what needs to be done or a lack of sufficient motivation. When the reward at the end of the task is not sufficient enough to motivate you to act, then the effort required always seems like it is too much. Laziness is not always a bad thing. Sometimes even the most hard-working people can experience burn out. When you reach this stage when you are physically and mentally exhausted, you probably feel like just taking a day off and doing nothing.

Everyone has days when all they want to do is stay in bed or lounge on the couch all day. Laziness sometimes can be your body's way of telling you to take it easy especially if you have been over-exerting yourself. When this happens a day of doing nothing may actually help you to recharge and clear your mind. However, habitual laziness is not just bad for your productivity but it can lead you to worse habits such as procrastination.

When you do not feel up to doing something, it means that you lack the motivation to put in the required effort. Laziness is mostly about a lack of clear goals or passion for what you need to do. When you are not clear about what you want or what you are working for, then it will be difficult to apply yourself to anything because well, it really does not matter to you. Unlike procrastination, laziness indicates a lack of purpose and passion.

Procrastinators on the other hand do have clear objectives, however, the execution of their plans becomes a problem due to emotional resistance. When you procrastinate it is due to poor planning, fear, indecision, and the inability to take action. Making the distinction between laziness and procrastination is important. It will help you to understand what is at the root of your inability to meet your goals. If your productivity is being impacted by laziness, then what you have is a lack of goals or the motivation to go after what you want.

The Pleasure Principle
Fast food, texting, social media, quickies, the list of things that we use to access pleasure swiftly is infinite. Human nature drives not just to seek pleasure but to seek pleasure *now*. Why feel good tomorrow if you can feel good now? Why take the long route if there is a shorter and easier shortcut? The psychology of instant gratification is simple; we want pleasure and we want it now.

The emotional discomfort associated with waiting for a reward is what overpowers your better judgment. Self-denial takes more than willpower; it requires self-discipline and unfortunately, this is where most people run into trouble. The pleasure principle as described by Sigmund Freud indicates that the unconscious mind is purely motivated by your baser instincts. These are the instincts that cause you to prioritize pleasure over discomfort no matter what the long-term consequences are likely to be.

Instant gratification is almost always self-defeating. Every time you choose pleasure, you are putting off something else that is more important and more relevant to your long-term goals. Instant gratification is one of the reasons why people tend to keep putting off things or delay working on them. When you end up spending hours on social media instead of doing your work, it is not that you do not know what the right thing is. It is because your need for pleasure is greater than your motivation to do your job.

How many times do you plan to be productive over the weekends only to end up sleeping in or binge-watching your favorite show? Do you keep planning to start on that new diet tomorrow? Do you find yourself always rushing to meet deadlines because you went out with your friends, again, instead of working on your project? The problem with instant gratification is that there is almost always something more fun, more interesting, and less challenging to do. If you get into a habit of always prioritizing pleasure the probability that you will be productive or reach your objectives is pretty minimal.

Putting on excess pounds, getting into debt, flunking your exams, messing up your career and many of the other pitfalls people get into are on some level connected to the need for instant gratification. People will max out their credit cards on things they cannot afford not because they are unaware of their financial situation, but because they lack the self-discipline to go against their need for instant gratification.

You will indulge in fast food even when you know what it is doing to your waistline and to your health. You see, when it comes to pleasure, you are fully aware of the consequences but you indulge the impulse nonetheless. Most addictive habits are borne out of the need to satisfy a craving in order to indulge your emotional impulses. Shopping makes you feel good so you keep doing it even when your finances are in the red. Ice cream comforts you when you are feeling low so you keep eating it even though you are trying to lose weight. You know your project is due tomorrow but you go out drinking because well, it is much more fun than working.

When you get into a habit of indulging your impulses with momentary pleasure you are succumbing to the pleasure principle. This habit can become so entrenched that it becomes difficult to beat. Addictions are a classic example of the self-defeating nature of instant gratification. Addicts struggle for years to overcome their addictions. This is not because they do not know the harm they are doing to themselves. Habits inevitably create loops in your brain that cannot be broken at the flip of a switch.

This loop starts with a trigger such as fear, anger, or any other emotion. Once you start to feel this negative emotion then you look for a way to feel better. This leads to the action. The action caused by the emotional trigger can be anything from shopping to binge eating or drinking. Once you act you start to feel good. This positive emotion is the reward. Essentially this creates a loop in your brain that leads from the trigger emotion to the action and finally to the reward.

Once these loops are entrenched in your brain, they happen almost on a subconscious level. Your baser instincts will drive your behavior because it is naturally inclined to seek pleasure and avoid discomfort. This becomes a problem for your productivity because in most cases there is no instant reward for work.

When you work hard today, there is no instant pleasure in that. The reward is somewhere off in the future and so the appeal in working hard cannot beat the allure of instant pleasure. In a nutshell, you will procrastinate and put things off more and more because you have gotten into a habit of giving in to the need for instant gratification.

The polar opposite of instant gratification is delayed gratification. In delayed gratification, you do the work today to reap the reward or benefits tomorrow. Your ability to prioritize delayed gratification over instant gratification will always be the key factor in whether or not you reach your goals. Both procrastinators and lazy people struggle with delayed gratification. They often lack the willpower to hold out and wait for the reward. If you fall into this category, chances are you are easily distracted and have trouble staying focused.

You may very well start on the task that you need to accomplish but if something else comes along that is more interesting or fun you will ditch what you were doing. That is why you will find that you end up with plenty of half-finished projects and tasks that you started but never completed. To beat procrastination, there is no getting around the fact that you have to train yourself to prioritize delayed gratification. This means staying dedicated to the task even when you would much rather be doing something else.

So how do you stop yourself from giving in to your baser instincts and staying on track? How do you stop your mind from wandering and keep yourself from distractions? To beat the need for instant gratification, you will need to shift your mind from constantly seeking pleasure. This means not just being self-aware but making a conscious effort to choose productivity over pleasure.

Like with any other habit, you will not eliminate the impulse for instant gratification overnight. However, the more you practice self-denial, the easier it gets with time. When you start seeing the fruits of your productivity, then the allure of momentary pleasure will pale in comparison to the idea of what you stand to gain.

Tips for overcoming procrastination through delayed gratification

- ***Have clear goals***

Waiting is hard in normal circumstances, but it can be even harder to do if you have no idea what it is you are waiting for. Without clear goals, you will always give in to your impulses because you do not have a higher purpose. Having a goal gives you something to aim for and work towards. This sense of purpose is what will help you keep things in perspective and prioritize the things that will really matter to you in the future.

Do not just show up at work to do what you are told to do. What are your personal goals? Do you want to move up the corporate ladder in two or three years? Do you want to acquire more skills? Do you want to save enough to start your own business or retire early? Do not just fall in line with other people's plans and objectives. Take time to find your own passions and goals and make them your bigger picture.

Often when you falter or lose sight of your goals it is because the goals you have are not meaningful enough to keep you committed. This happens when you are just going along with other people's ideas and plans. Having goals will not only point you in the right direction but it keeps you focused on the important things in your life. Set clear goals for your finances, your health, your career, your relationships, and everything else that is important to you.

When you have a goal, you create a plan to help you get to the goal. Once you have this plan then you will be less tempted to give in to your impulses. A plan makes the right path clear. You are less likely to go on a shopping spree if you have set a goal to save for something important like college or your first home. Goals give you purpose and purpose makes the wait worthwhile.

If you are constantly getting distracted and looking for ways to indulge your impulses, this just means that your goals are either non-existent or not meaningful enough to you. Make goals for each area of your life based on where you want to be in a month, a year or five from now. What do you really want? Once you have these goals then ask yourself what you need to do today, and each day until you achieve them.

When you are clear on your purpose then even when you procrastinate or give in to laziness it will only be a momentary lapse. Goals serve as a beacon that lights your way forward and shows you exactly where it you need to go. Once you know where you are going then the steps that you need to take become more or less self-explanatory.

- ***Take control of your environment***

Out of sight out of mind is a good motto especially if you find that you get easily distracted. To be productive you have to consciously cultivate an environment that enables rather than hinders you. Why would you keep your phone near you when trying to complete an important project? Why make needless trips to the mall if you know that once you start shopping you cannot stop yourself?

Just like an addict tells themselves they can stop anytime they want; you can sabotage yourself by not acknowledging your weakness. Telling yourself that you will only look at your Instagram feed for five minutes or that you will only hit one shop is setting yourself up for failure. If you know the things that distract you, keep away from them until you have completed the task at hand.

Switch off your phone or have it muted when working on important projects. If you have trouble sticking to a budget, have someone else do the shopping or buy your stuff online so you do not get tempted to buy things you do not need. Smart people know their weaknesses and smarter people make sure to stay away from temptation. Do not try to test your willpower by keeping distractions in sight. Chances are if you remove the things that tempt you from sight, you will have an easier time staying focused.

If you want to go on diet, you do not stock up your fridge with all kinds of junk food. Instead, you stock up on healthy stuff so that even if you are tempted to indulge you only have healthy food. This kind of planning helps you to stay committed to your goals by making sure your environment is working for you. Keep the temptations away and there will be fewer distractions taking you away from what is important.

Distractions also apply to the kind of people you surround yourself with. Do not expect to go too far if you are always hanging out with people who have no goals of their own. You want to have people who will push you to be better and help you work towards your goals. Make sure that the kind of friends you have are building you up and not tearing you down. This does not mean that you need to have identical goals with your friends. It simply means that the people in your life should not be the ones hindering you from moving forward.

Just like a plant needs to be nurtured in the right environment to grow so do you. You would not plant a seed on a bed of rocks or in a dark corner where it does not get any light or water. A seed will only grow if it has the right balance of light, water, and nutrition to keep it nurtured.

If you have done any kind of gardening, then you know that plants always grow towards the sun or the light. This is because they look for what nurtures and helps them to grow. This is a valuable lesson that you can use to know which direction to grow in. Seek out the people, the situations, and the environment that nurture you and help you to thrive; that is your sun.

- **_Think things through_**

Impulses are the things that lead you to seek instant gratification. When you have an impulse, you rarely think it through. This is because your baser instincts drive your emotional brain and your emotions drive your behavior. When you do not take time to think things through, instant gratification will always seem like a good idea.

Weighing the pros and cons before you make decisions can help you overcome procrastination and beat the impulse to prioritize pleasure. Take a minute to ask yourself, *if I do this now what will it mean tomorrow? If I do not finish this project today, what will my boss think of me? If I skip the lecture how will that affect my performance, if I eat fast food, how will I ever get back in shape?* These kinds of questions help you see the consequences of your actions. They will give you some perspective and help you figure out what is more important.

Pausing for a minute before you choose or act can help you overcome your emotional impulses. Why is it that with the benefit of hindsight you can clearly see where you went wrong? It is simply because once you have had a chance to think things through you understand them better. Impulses are usually strong if you do not stop to question them or think them through.

You are craving a nice juicy burger, so you go out and get one. Rarely do you stop to think, *why a burger, not a salad or something healthy?* You simply do what you feel like and leave the consequences to take care of themselves. If you were to flip the script and start by thinking of the consequences before you act, I am pretty sure you would make a lot of different choices.

Self-denial is not so difficult when you have a clear idea of the cost of instant gratification. Take time to think things through before acting. Weigh what you stand to gain versus what you stand to lose. If a few minutes of pleasure are going to cost you your goals, then they are probably not worth it.

- ***Delay the reward***

Following through on your goals does not mean you cannot have any fun. It simply means rewarding yourself after the work is done not before you do the work. Reward yourself after accomplishing a task or doing what you are supposed to. When you learn to delay gratification, it essentially becomes your motivation to finish the task.

Instead of going for a movie and putting off your schoolwork, how about you reward yourself with a movie after finishing the school work? When you make the reward come after the work you will enjoy it so much more because there is no guilt involved. Nothing is as pleasant as the feeling you get when you know that you have dotted all your I's and crossed all your t's.

To beat procrastination, you do not need to stop doing all the things you enjoy. You simply need to switch up your priorities so that the work comes before the fun. Delayed gratification lasts longer, costs you less, and teaches you that waiting for a reward is well worth the effort.

The next time you are tempted to put off your work or an important task, ask yourself what it would feel like after you have finished. Envision completing the task and how it will feel. When you can visualize the outcome, the reward does not seem so far-fetched.

The trouble with instant gratification is that it is fleeting. You never really enjoy it as much as you thought because there is always something that needs to be done hanging over your head. Delay the pleasure and make it the reward you get after finishing whatever it is that you need to do.

Investing in the Process
You want to be financially stable, but you still want to spend money. You want to be fit and healthy but you still want to eat whatever you want. You want to get promoted but you also want to put in as little effort as possible. Having your cake and eating it too may be the best of both worlds but in reality, it does not happen. You have to choose one or the other.

To beat procrastination and even laziness, the process has to be as important if not more important than the result. Let's say you set out to lose some weight and give yourself a month to do it. The first week you are as good as gold. Only healthy food, reasonable portions, and plenty of exercise. You are excited and motivated to reach your goal. At the end of the week, you get on the scale and you have only lost half a pound.

This minuscule progress disappoints you and you cannot figure out why after all the hard work you have nothing to show for it. Nonetheless, you keep going and in the second week, you work even harder. You increase your exercises, eat less, and stay focused on your goal. At the end of the second week, you get on the scale, and to your horror, you have actually gained a pound. This takes all the wind out of your sails and you start to think maybe it's just your genes and you are destined to be overweight.

By this time, you are completely discouraged and you either stop following your diet program or keep going half-heartedly. At some point, you go back to your old ways because after all your hard work you have nothing to show for it. This scenario happens many times over in our lives. It doesn't matter what the goal is. It could be a promotion, a new job, better grades, or a new relationship.

Whatever the goal is, you will start off determined and committed. However, the longer you go without seeing any results, the more you start to lose your dedication. This is because it is human nature to prioritize the result over the process. When you think about your goals, you think about them in terms of what you are going to get; not what you have to do to get it.

When you focus only on the result without investing in the process, you will often falter and give up halfway through whatever you are doing. This is because in your mind you do not appreciate the value of the process. You want the result but you want it now, you do not want to have to wait for it. The trouble with this mindset is that in most cases the process is more important than the result. No matter how long it takes, if you get the process right then the result will take care of itself.

Stop looking at your goal as an end in itself but as part of a process that helps you to go from where you are now to where you want to be. For instance, to achieve financial independence you may have to teach yourself to save, live within your means, and to invest wisely. These lessons may not be what you are aiming for but they will serve you even after you achieve your goal. This is why it is important to value the process that takes you to your goals.

If your goal is to lose weight, you will need to eat healthier, exercise more, and be more conscious of your health. Even after you lose the weight, you will still need these lessons to stay fit and healthy. The process doesn't just get you to the goal but it helps you sustain and keep the progress you have made. Yo-yo dieters keep gaining back the weight they have lost because they do not value the process. Once they get to their goal, they forget the lessons and go back to their old ways.

When you invest in the process, your focus is not on the result but on the steps that you need to take to get to the result. Valuing the process helps you keep your faith when things are tough. It helps you to stay committed and disciplines you to stay on track. When you are tied to your goals by self-discipline you are more likely to achieve them than if you were just going off of emotion or motivation.

Stop thinking about the outcome and focus on the plan of action. When your mind is on what you need to do today, then you will have no time to worry about the possibility of failure. Investing in the process pushes you to act because you know exactly what needs to be done and when it needs to be done. Once you have set your goal, shift your focus to the plan of action. Set out deliberate steps and actions that you will use to build the habits that will get you to your goal.

If it seems like you will never get the promotion, forget about the promotion for now and focus on doing a good job today. Make sure that your work is exceptional. Step up and take on challenges whenever the opportunity arises. Make yourself invaluable by being good at what you do and great at seizing opportunities. Whether or not you eventually get the promotion, you will have become better at your job. Your power is not in what may or may not happen, but rather in the actions that you are taking today.

If you are a student, instead of always fretting about your GPA, focus on studying and passing your exams. The process is what ensures the result so it should be the most important thing when going after your goals. The problem with focusing too much on the result is that it makes it easy to procrastinate. When the result seems so far off, you get discouraged, and staying committed becomes difficult.

Every goal is going to seem impossible if you look at it with an all or nothing perspective. Focus on the steps and let the end game take care of itself. It is not about the 40 pounds that you need to lose, it is about eating right today and getting in some exercise. It is not about impressing your boss so that you get a promotion, it is about turning in exemplary work that speaks for itself. Without the process, the result is not possible.

Mastering Self-regulation

"Unless you make the unconscious conscious, it will direct your life and you will call it fate." C. Jung

How often do you feel like the world is against you or like you are struggling to row against the tide? It is not uncommon to feel like there is some invisible force out to get you. Your boss doesn't like you; your colleague is always sabotaging you, and the traffic always seems much worse when you are running late. All this may be true, but how often do you stop to think how much of the bad luck in your life is your own doing?

It is often much easier to look for solutions externally because looking inward requires you to question your belief and your values. When you cannot cultivate self-awareness then there is very little chance that you will learn to self-regulate. You must be willing to confront your beliefs and values in order to master self-regulation.

Self-regulation is the ability to control your emotions and impulses. It is self-regulation that will enable you to say no to a night out when you have important work to do. Self-regulation means that you can feel tempted to put off something but not give in to the feeling. In other words, self-control is what makes the difference between emotional thinking and rational thinking.

Emotional thinking is the purview of the limbic system of the brain. This part of your brain is where emotions are generated. Any time you have an interaction, a thought, or an experience, your limbic system is the first point of interpretation. This means that your brain interprets things emotionally before it can interpret them rationally. This gives emotions an upper hand in directing our behavior and actions.

Our emotional nature is what makes the need for instant gratification so hard to overcome. Think of it this way, every time you put off doing something, it is not because you do not know that it is important but rather because you do not *feel* like doing it. Emotions can be a powerful motivator and unless you learn how to self-regulate you will always be a prisoner to your impulses.

To overcome the natural inclination to prioritize pleasure and overcome procrastination, self-regulation is key. You have to master self-denial and learn to do things not because they feel good but because they are important. Your better judgment should always carry the day when trying to choose which way to go. This does not mean that you will not have any emotions. Self-regulation means that you have emotions just like anyone else but they are not the driving force behind why you do things.

Tips for mastering self-regulation

Cultivate self-awareness

Know your weaknesses. If you are easily distracted by your phone or music anything else, make sure this distraction is nowhere in sight when you have an important task to accomplish. Know the triggers that cause you to procrastinate or put off doing things.

When you know where your blind spots are, it becomes so much easier to fight them. Being self-aware makes it much easier to process and deal with negative emotions. When you are tempted to put off something important, ask yourself why. Is it because you are scared of the outcome? Are you doubting your ability? Is it simply laziness? When you question your emotions, you begin to unravel their hold on you.

Everyone has weaknesses but those who know what their weaknesses are better equipped to overcome them. Stay in tune with your inner thoughts and emotions and you will unravel the real reasons why you procrastinate.

Strive to be present

A lot of procrastination is driven by your fears of the future or regrets about the past. Living in the moment helps you to control your emotions by shutting down the mental experiences. Mental experiences are thoughts about the past or the future that take your focus away from the present. Learn to live in the moment without overthinking either your past or your future.

Your fears can be totally unrelated to your current situation but they will stop you in your tracks nonetheless. This is because emotions affect your mental clarity and prevent you from seeing things objectively. When you start to judge your present based on your past, then chances are you will always feel overwhelmed and intimidated by challenges. This means that to make progress you need to leave your emotional baggage behind and live in the moment.

Practices like meditation and breathing exercises can help you to process negative emotions. When you practice mindfulness techniques you effectively bring your focus back to the present and this helps you to manage negative emotions.

Have a plan

Emotional impulses will only derail you if you do not have a plan. Stop waiting for motivation or inspiration to strike. Create schedules and timetables that prompt you to act and get moving. Your day should be purposeful and directed by a goal or plan that needs to be accomplished.

Simply having a to-do list or a schedule can help you stay on track. It is much harder to give in to your impulses when you have created a plan and schedule for yourself. When you get up in the morning ask yourself what you need to accomplish that day. Go further and actually write it down. No matter what mood you are in, you will have set yourself tasks to accomplish. This will help you to overcome any emotional resistance to what you need to do.

Self-control is understanding that you have emotions and that to overcome them you need something bigger than those emotions. A plan gives you purpose and direction. It makes it easier to say no to temptation and distractions.

Chapter 5: Get A Grip

The Emotional Nature of Procrastination
By and large, humans are pretty simple beings. We feel, then we think and then we act. It's just the way we are wired. Our emotional brain is faster than our rational brain and so most of the decisions we make are driven by emotions. When you are trying to figure out why it takes you so damn long to get off your ass and do the things you know you need to be doing, you cannot overlook the emotional aspect of procrastination.

Our emotions fall into two broad categories. There are positive feelings such as joy, excitement, pride, gratitude and then there are negative emotions like fear, shame, guilt, and anger. Every time you are faced with a task or a decision, it can either be associated with positive emotions or with negative emotions.

If an activity brings you pleasure or a sense of pride in accomplishing it then it becomes a source of positive emotions and you want to do it more and more. For instance, if you are good at creating winning proposals at work, then every time you have such a project you will approach it with enthusiasm and confidence. The same goes for activities you enjoy like hanging out with friends, watching your favorite show, and so on. You will always prioritize tasks that make you feel good.

On the other hand, some things challenge you and make you uncomfortable. If you have a difficult task like going for an interview or sitting for an exam, you are likely to experience negative emotions like anxiety or dread. In this case, you may go out of your way to postpone the experience or avoid it together because of the negative emotions. Naturally, the things that we have positive emotional reactions to are easier to do than those things that elicit negative emotions in us. In essence, most of the things that you procrastinate about are things that have a negative emotion associated with them.

If you are afraid you will fail let's say at an interview, of course, you will not be eager to get to it. You may even find ways to avoid putting yourself in that situation where you will be judged by others. When tasks or decisions become associated with negative emotions, then you will have no enthusiasm for them. You will find excuses to not do them or to keep postponing them. This is because negative emotions threaten our sense of security and because we do not like to feel uncomfortable we find ways to avoid them.

Have you ever stopped to wonder why people are constantly complaining about their jobs, their financial situations, their love life, and everything in between? People complain because they know what the problem is, they know that it can be fixed but they are unwilling to effect the change. Why you may ask? Because the fear of putting yourself out there, taking a risk, or leaving your comfort zone far outweighs the discomfort of being in an unhappy situation.

The reason why most people never reach their goals is not that they do not know what they need to do, but rather because they lack the courage to do it. It may be a cliché but the truth is, everything you have ever wanted lives on the other side of your fear. This means that if you are to overcome procrastination, you must first be able to conquer your emotions and self-regulate.

Emotions are a powerful driving force and unless you can control your emotions then you will have very little control over your life. Getting a grip means that you are not letting your emotions drive your decisions and that you have control over the choices you make. Naturally, emotions are at the core of the human experience so you cannot avoid having emotions both good and bad. However, when you have control over these emotions you will be capable of feeling them but not making decisions based on them.

So the next time you put off working on that assignment or applying for a job you want or even asking out the person you have a crush on, ask yourself, *why am I hesitating? am I afraid I will fail? am I afraid I will succeed? Am I afraid of change?* When you start to self-examine the reasons why you keep putting things off you will start to unravel the emotions that are holding you hostage.

It does not matter what kind of procrastinator you are. Whether you are the perfectionist, the pleasure seeker, or even the dreamer, you will realize that nine times out of ten you put things off because of emotional reasons, not logical ones. You avoid working on something because you do not *feel* motivated, or you do not want to talk to your boss about a raise because you are *afraid* of what he will say or you do not want to go to the gym because you *hate* working out.

Emotional resistance is the strongest deterrent to getting things done. Unless you can get a grip over your emotions than you will always find that you prioritize things that make you feel good and put off the things that scare or challenge you in some way. Emotional decisions are the surest way to get off track and lose sight of your goals because as we all know the things that feel good are not always the best things for us.

If you have trouble with regulating your emotions, start by cultivating self-awareness. Most of the time when emotions get the better of you, its because you are not really in touch with what you are feeling or what is causing that particular feeling. For instance, your fear of doing something challenging may really just be due to a lack of self-confidence or an unwillingness to test your skills.

Switch off the autopilot and delve behind the emotion to find the why. More often than not you will find that your triggers for negative emotions are hangovers from past mistakes and have nothing to do with the situation you are currently in. Before you think *oh no, I will do this tomorrow,* or *ill work on this later,* look behind the emotion. Why are you avoiding that task or decision? Do you have a logical reason or are you simply going off your emotions? The more you understand your emotions the more manageable they will be.

The Curse of Inaction

So, you have been putting off doing something for a while now. Every time you think about it, you push it to the back of your mind. You are waiting to work up the nerve to do it or for just the right moment. Unfortunately, the more you put off doing something, the scarier and more challenging it gets.

The longer you wait, the more daunting the task or decision becomes. It goes from being this thing you do not like and morphs into this larger than life challenge. Inaction is one of the surest ways to make mountains out of molehills. This increasing fear is because inaction breeds more doubt and more fear. Eventually, the fear becomes so great that you may talk yourself out of doing what you need to or wait until the very last minute to do it.

This is the curse of inaction the more you sit with your dread the bigger it becomes. The opposite is true with action. When you start working on something, your confidence increases and you end up feeling more motivated to continue. This means that inaction becomes a self-propagating cycle where you are too afraid to act so you do not start and because you do not start your fear only keeps on growing.

The only difference between procrastinators and proactive people is that people who are proactive feel the fear but take the first step anyway. They understand that after the first step, the fear starts to dissipate until they are no longer afraid. Action breeds confidence while inaction breeds doubt and fear. One way or the other, the one you choose will determine not just how productive you are but whether or not you can achieve your goals.

Think of someone who needs to get up in front of a group of people and give a speech. Before the speech, they will be nervous and dreading getting up on the stage. When they get to the podium, they will probably falter in the first two or three sentences, but after that, they will get into the moment and their confidence will gradually increase as they keep speaking. Ultimately, the only way to overcome your fear is to act. The cure for fear is not avoiding action but rather to take the first step.

Once you realize that action breeds confidence, then even the most daunting task becomes manageable. This means that to get past your inaction, all you need to do is start. You do not have to figure everything out in the beginning, just make your first step, and gradually the process gets easier as you go along. Often when something seems challenging or larger than life, we keep avoiding it because it seems too daunting. However, when you break it down into small steps then you find that you can tackle it bit by bit.

Break down the process into bite-sized pieces. For instance, if you have been sitting with a book idea for years. You do not have to have the whole plot figured out. Start with the first line, then the next paragraph and slowly you will find your rhythm and no matter what comes next, nothing will be as hard as putting down that first sentence.

This principle applies to any situation. For example, if you need to eat healthier or lose some weight, focus on the first step. Do not try to do everything all at once. Start with one step then work your way down until everything you need to do gets done. The first step could be getting rid of all the junk food in your fridge or signing up for a gym membership. Once the first step is done, then the rest of the steps become clearer and you are no longer looking up at an insurmountable mountain.

Why Tomorrow is Too Late
What's the big deal? After all, it does not matter if you do it today or tomorrow right? Wrong, it actually does matter because productivity happens on a timeline. Your boss will give you a task to finish by a certain time, or you will need to apply for that job you have always wanted while there is still a vacancy. Time makes all the difference when it comes to productivity and achieving your goals. To beat procrastination, you need to understand the value of now, and why tomorrow is never good enough.

Time management is one of the surest ways to get past your inaction and to start doing the things you need to be doing now, not tomorrow or later, or sometime in the future. For people who struggle with procrastination, one of the most effective time management techniques is the Pomodoro technique. This technique helps you to tackle your tasks and increase your productivity in five easy steps.

Here is how to use the Pomodoro technique works:

1. Pick a specific task to work on. Be specific on what exactly you want to do. Set a clear task like, *work on the introduction for my thesis*, or *work on five items from my in-tray*.

2. Focus on the task for at least 25 minutes. This means paying full undivided attention to the task you have specified.

3. If you find your mind wandering from the task. Write down the intrusive thoughts on paper. Writing down your distractions actually helps you to stop them from running through your mind constantly.

4. After the 25 minutes are over, take a break. You can stretch for five minutes, get yourself some water, or just walk around for five minutes. This break helps you to stay focused without feeling overwhelmed or exhausted.

5. After your break, get back to your task and keep following the steps until you have finished what you set out to do in step 1.

Overcoming your Fear
Fear is the common denominator that underlies all types of procrastination. Whether it is the fear of failure, the fear of change, the fear of being judged, or even the fear of success, procrastination starts with fear at its core. So without understanding what is causing your fear and overcoming it, you will always have moments where you are paralyzed into inaction because you are afraid.

For most people, when they think of fear their minds immediately go to this overwhelming dread that a person feels when they are in mortal peril or let's say being chased by a bear. However, fear is not always a result of a physical threat or even real physical danger. Fear can also be caused by negative thoughts, your imagination, and even your beliefs. This means that fear does not have to be real or factual, in most cases, your fear is nothing more than you giving in to your self-limiting beliefs.

For instance, if John wants to ask Claire out on a date for the first time. First, he thinks *oh I really like Claire I should ask her out for coffee*, then that thought is followed by, *what is the best way to ask her?*, and then after that thought he thinks, *I bet she will say no, why would she like me I am just a nerd and she is so....* Now by the time John finishes this last thought, he has already gone from simply wanting to ask Claire out to imagining she will turn him down. Naturally, once the negative thoughts set in, John will put off asking Claire out or avoid doing it altogether because he is afraid of being turned down.

This is just a simple illustration of how we create and feed our own fears through our self-limiting beliefs and thoughts. In John's case, he has no idea what Claire will really say if he asks her out but he has already come up with the worst-case scenario based on what he thinks of himself. His fear is all internally generated and has nothing to do with the other person. This is the reason why procrastination can be so debilitating. It starts with our own self-limiting beliefs and often has nothing to do with the thing that you are afraid to do.

So how do you overcome this emotional fear? Well, the first step is to identify your own self-limiting beliefs. Are you dreading that assignment because you do not have confidence in yourself? Are you afraid to ask for a raise because you secretly think you don't deserve it? or, are you staying in a toxic relationship because you are afraid of change? Whatever self-limiting belief you have about yourself, understand where it is coming from.

For most people, their beliefs are based on a past experience or even something someone told them. If we go back to our example, maybe John thinks he is a nerd because someone once told him, *you are such a nerd*. So, he took this opinion and based his beliefs on who he is on that. Now this belief stops him from going after what he wants because it is a self-limiting label that makes him feel that he is flawed in some way. Even when your beliefs are based on past experience, they are not necessarily factual and should not form the basis on which you judge your capability or strengths.

Imagine someone who was cheated on by a former partner and then this person starts to believe that there is something wrong with them or that they are not good enough. This belief will affect their ability to approach any relationship from a healthy emotional space. This means that every chance to be with someone else will just feel like an opportunity to be hurt again and so slowly they will start dreading relationships. They will base their feelings on relationships on one bad experience and inadvertently become wary and cynical about relationships.

In essence, to overcome your fear, you must fast strip away all the labels you have placed on yourself. Instead of being a nerd asking a girl out, just be a guy asking a girl out. Instead of being the salesman who always screws up the presentation, just be a salesman. When you stop labeling your failures and your past mistakes and making them who you are, then you give yourself a chance to approach any task from a positive frame of mind. Self-limiting beliefs will have power over you if you use them to define who you are.

Define yourself in the simplest way possible. If you are constantly intimidating yourself with your beliefs and the labels you have created for yourself you will never get anything done. Remember that most of the fear that causes you to procrastinate is nothing more than an opinion or belief you have created in your mind that tells you, you can't or you shouldn't.

Chapter 6: The Octopus Myth

Does your daily life feel like it's a juggling act where you have to keep a dozen different balls up in the air? Are you constantly frazzled, rushed, stressed, and short on time? When it comes to keeping up with the demands of a high-pressure home and work environment, it is very easy to start overextending yourself. This is when your plate is so full you barely have any free time for yourself.

In the natural scheme of things, you would assume that being busy and being productive are the same thing but actually, you would be wrong. People who take on more than they can handle end up running themselves into the ground and reducing their overall efficiency. In fact, studies into neuron function have shown that multi-tasking tends to reduce brain efficiency. This means that when you are doing too much, even tasks that are not too demanding become challenging. This is because you are overextended and unable to focus on any one particular task.

Doing too much is not just bad for your stress levels but is actually one of the major causes of procrastination. When you are overwhelmed with dozens of things to do, it is no surprise that you can barely find time to do the things that are really important. Think of all the days you show up at work determined to get things done only to spend most of the day responding to emails or in crisis meetings. Sometimes you do not procrastinate because you are afraid of the challenge but rather because you fail to prioritize your tasks.

Every day you will have dozens of things that need to get done, but it is up to you to decide which of these things are relevant to your goals and which are simply busywork. The trouble with taking on too much is that often the little unimportant things end up taking up so much of your energy that you have little time left to deal with the important stuff. This leads to a situation where you are always trying to keep up with your responsibilities because you never have enough time to get everything done.

Essentially procrastination becomes a self-perpetuating cycle. The things you did not handle today become urgent tomorrow and the things you were meant to do tomorrow have to be postponed. This then becomes your life, playing catch up and always under pressure. In such situations, you will go to bed totally exhausted at the end of each day but with little to show for it. This maximum effort minimum results scenario is not just frustrating but can also lead to stress and burnout.

The irony in procrastination is that you may actually be one of the busiest people you know; so how come you get so little done? On the surface, you know that you are not just lazing around all day but you always end up with lots of tasks that did not get done, projects that are overdue, and deadlines that need to be met. What you do not realize is that it is very easy to substitute efficiency for busyness.

Efficiency means that you are accomplishing the important tasks while busyness simply means that you are working. To be efficient you must be doing the important things first and then the not so important tasks. When you procrastinate, you have a pile of urgent things to attend to. These things are urgent because they are late, not because they are important. In this way, the urgent gets in the way of the important and so you are always busy but on the whole not very productive.

The Curse of Urgent

Where did the time go? Is a common question that procrastinators find themselves asking at the end of the day. You look back at your week and you were as busy and as hardworking as ever. So how come you are as far from your goal on Friday as you were on Monday? The simple answer is that you often ignore the important tasks to deal with the urgent. Think of the little things that keep cropping up in the course of the day that demand your immediate attention. You do not plan for them but they end up taking up most of your time.

The curse of urgent is that it causes you to ignore important tasks and actions. When you are preoccupied with things that require immediate attention but are not important, your energy and time are taken away from the goals you should be focused on.

Let's say you show up at the office with your to-do list for the day determined to be productive. Before you get started on your task, an email from your client comes in complaining about something or other. You then start following up with other departments to find out what happened or try to placate the client in some other way. Before you know it, half the day is gone and most of it has been spent on something that was not on your to-do list.

As you attend to yesterday's crisis and put out fires from things that were ignored yesterday, the things you were supposed to do today become crises for tomorrow. This self-perpetuating cycle is what makes it so hard to get back on track once you have been derailed by tasks that may be urgent but not important. This means that to avoid procrastination that stems from doing too much you must learn to separate the vital few from the trivial many.

Having a clear understanding of what tasks need to be done now and which ones can be done later is probably one of the most important things you can do for your productivity. Effort does not always equal result and that is why working smart is more important than working hard. Running yourself ragged will do you no good if all you are focusing on are the urgent but not the really important tasks.

People who stay productive know not just how to prioritize but also how to say no. Saying no to unimportant tasks means that you can say yes to the things that are relevant to your goals.

Trying to balance a dozen different things at once will only distract you from your goals. Before you plan your day, think of what tasks are most important in terms of getting you closer to your goals and which tasks can be delegated and done later. You may feel that doing everything yourself makes you more productive but in actual sense, productive people only focus on what is important. They are not afraid to delegate or say no when they have too much on their plate.

When you are constantly under pressure, you create a situation where it is easy to put off important things because you simply do not have the time or energy to take them on. You may even feel like you cannot take on something. Yet, the truth is that, if you had more time to work on it, you could probably handle it just fine. This is the curse of urgent. It breeds the perfect environment for procrastination. You never really know where your time goes or why you are putting in so much effort for minimal results.

To beat the curse of urgent you must first recognize all the things that take up your time yet they are not actually important. How often do you say yes to tasks that you really do not have time for just to please others? How many times do you get derailed by a mini-crisis that was not even on your to-do list? Is the effort your putting in equal to the result you are getting? Analyze how you prioritize tasks and which kind of tasks take up the lion's share of your time. This information will help you figure out why you are falling behind on the important tasks because you are too preoccupied with the urgent.

Haste and urgency lead you down a path of maximum effort for little results. You will always be busy but you will never have anything solid to show for all the work that you are doing. You will always be on the wrong side of the clock playing catch up. The curse of urgent will always leave you feeling like you are busy running on a treadmill that is essentially getting you nowhere.

Tips for prioritizing and getting things done

- ***Be real with yourself***

Stop trying to be superwoman or superman. You cannot do everything and do it all well. Knowing what your limits are is important. A lot of times people take on more than they can handle to prove something to themselves or others. Running yourself down is not going to do you or anyone else much good. Be honest with yourself about what is just enough and what is too much.

If you are constantly stressed out, exhausted, and always short on time, it is time to re-evaluate how much you are taking on. Realize that when you stretch yourself too thin, important stuff slips through the cracks and you start to lose sight of your goals. Be kind to yourself by allowing yourself the time and mental reserves you need to do the things that really matter.

Do not be afraid to admit you need help. Delegate tasks if you need to. Decline to take up extra projects if your plate is already full and always prioritize the tasks that are important. When you prioritize, you ensure that even if you run out of time the most important things will have been accomplished.

- ***Stop multi-tasking***

Life moves at a frantic pace and sometimes it becomes necessary to juggle more than one task. As much as you may feel like you are saving time by multi-tasking, you are also reducing your overall efficiency. When you multi-task, it is easy to get overwhelmed and make simple mistakes that end up costing you even more time.

Allocate time for each task then work on it until it is done before moving on to the next one. This will keep you focused on one task at a time enabling you to not just finish the task but also do it well. Stop pushing things forward because they are too hard. Procrastinating only means that you will have more urgent things to do tomorrow. Make the most important tasks the first thing you do no matter how challenging they are.

- ***Take regular breaks***

Do not overwork yourself. When you wear yourself out you just make it difficult to stay focused on your goal. Take regular breaks in between your work to help you recharge and de-stress. Trying to work for 8 hours straight may seem like it will get you more results but ultimately a tired mind is not really that efficient. Short walks, a water break, or simply stretching every hour or so will help you to keep your brain functioning at optimum levels.

Schedule your work in such a way that you have some downtime to clear your mind and relax every so often. When you are under too much pressure you will find that you have trouble concentrating. This ultimately slows you down and makes you less efficient.

- ***Save the important tasks for your most productive time***

Some people are morning persons, others are night owls and some function best in the evenings. Whatever your most productive time is, use it to work on the most important tasks. Identify which of the time you feel the most productive and mentally sharp. If you are most productive in the mornings, then start your day by working on the most important tasks. If you are more of a night owl, save the meaningful tasks for that time of day.

Tapping into your body's natural potential helps you save time and effort. Use the times when you are less efficient to do simpler tasks or just take that time to relax and recharge. Remember working smart beats working hard.

Managing Stress and Burnout

It is common to hear people who procrastinate say, *I work best under pressure*. When people say this, they mean that they are at their most efficient when they are being pushed by a sense of urgency or looming deadline. This kind of high-pressure environment may be the shove that some people need to get off their ass and get moving. However, for most people pressure simply leads to stress, and the more stressed they become the lower the productivity sinks.

When you procrastinate one of the things that become a constant fixture in your life is stress. When you are always playing catch up and trying to beat the clock, the amount of pressure in your life keeps increasing. Looming deadlines, overdue bills, late submissions, and the ever-present possibility of falling short are the perfect recipe for high levels of stress. With stress comes reduced productivity, emotional distress, and a general inability to cope with the pressures of life.

Managing stress is essential to maintaining mental clarity and focus. It will also help to reduce the inclination to put off things because you are too stressed out to work on them. The tricky thing about stress is that it can become such an intrinsic part of your life that you do not even realize that you are living with it. The first step in stress management is therefore to first identify whether you are living with stress.

Stress often goes hand in hand with burn out. Burn out is usually a symptom that you are mentally, physically, and emotionally exhausted. This happens commonly when you are doing too much or when you have reached a point where you are not making any progress. Stress and burn out tend to lead to disillusionment, lack of interest or motivation, and a general feeling of emptiness. Burn out is usually associated with chronic stress and is not only a productivity issue but may also lead to health issues.

How do you know you are suffering from burn-out?

Chronic exhaustion

Do you ever go to bed tired, wake up tired, and spend the whole day just feeling utterly exhausted? Chronic exhaustion is one of the classic signs of burn-out. This kind of exhaustion has little to do with your physical state which is why you feel it even when you have just gotten out of bed.

When you are chronically tired all the time for no apparent reason, this means that you have reached the point of burn out.

Lack of motivation

Another sign of burn out is that you are utterly devoid of motivation. You lose interest in everything and you really do not care what happens one way or the other. You will find people who were passionate and enthusiastic about their work suddenly have no interest and cannot summon up any enthusiasm for their work at all. When you are burnt out, you are emotionally tapped out so even summoning the motivation needed to pursue your goals is impossible.

Inability to concentrate

You can stare at a computer screen for hours without really making sense of anything or doing anything productive. Chronic stress and burnout impair mental clarity and make it difficult for you to focus. If you suddenly find that tasks that were quite easy for you have suddenly become challenging, you may be suffering from burn out.

Erratic moods

If you go from ecstatic one minute to anxious the next, this is another symptom of burnout. Chronic stress and burnout tend to wreak havoc on your emotions and you never really know what you are feeling or why. You become prone to emotional outbursts and erratic mood swings. This kind of mood swings impair your productivity and start to affect your relationships with others.

Your performance changes drastically

Burn out can have a dramatic effect on your performance and ability to work. Since your mental focus is no longer as sharp your productivity suffers and the resulting effect on your performance can be drastic. Stellar students can flunk their exams due to burnout and exemplary employees can lose their jobs as a result of burnout. If your performance has suddenly taken a downturn and you are not sure why it may be time to check for other signs of chronic stress and burnout.

Health issues

Chronic stress can decrease your body's ability to fight off infections making you prone to health issues. You will find that you keep coming down with all sorts of bugs and you are constantly battling ailments. This ill-health can signal the effect of chronic stress on your body's immunity. If you have underlying health conditions, stress can exacerbate them and make them worse. Conditions such as hypertension, heart disease, and inflammatory conditions have been linked to chronic stress.

Tips for dealing with stress and burn out

1) Make time for yourself

When you are constantly running yourself down with unending work, responsibilities, and chores, burn out is inevitable. Taking time to breathe and recharge is not just essential for your productivity but also for your health. If you are constantly running on empty, you need to make time for yourself.

Allocate yourself some quiet time each day to just wind down and recharge. Do something you enjoy with this time or simply relax and let your mind rest. Resist the urge to work for hours on end without breaks. Your time is only used efficiently when you are able to concentrate and focus. Take breaks in between tasks and give your mind a breather from time to time.

Have some interests outside work that will help to keep you emotionally balanced. Hobbies, friends and even just spending time with your family can be a great way to ease the constant pressure of work. Make it a point to have a life outside of work and fill it with the things and people you love.

One of the reasons you procrastinate is because you feel overwhelmed and mentally exhausted. When you make time for yourself, you reassert some level of control over your life and this gives you the confidence to take on even challenging tasks. Taking care of yourself just makes you better equipped to make the decisions you need to make and take action when required.

2) Focus on the progress

Stress usually starts building up when you feel like you are doing all the work but not necessarily getting anything done. This can cause you to feel demotivated and make you lose interest in your goals. The only way to beat the feeling of hopelessness is by focusing on the small milestones and noting the progress you are making.

A lot of times people look at goals with an all or nothing perspective. This means that if you have not achieved it yet, you chalk it up as a failure. With this kind of perspective, you forget to appreciate the progress you are making and this causes you to feel disillusioned and like you have failed in some way. Take time to appreciate the little milestones and the victories you get along the way. a positive outlook gives you the strength to keep you going and helps you to stay motivated.

When pursuing your goals, it is important to remember that the process is every bit as important as your goal. Be your own cheerleader and appreciate the progress you are making even if you have not quite reached where you want to go. When you celebrate the small victories, you get the self-belief to keep going and stay committed to your long-term goal.

People procrastinate when they cannot see the possibility of success. It is not always about the end goal, the progress that you make on the way to the goal is equally important.

3) Have a daily wind-down ritual

If you procrastinate a lot, they often you will find yourself with a never-ending list of things that need to get done. This is because when you procrastinate you are forced to be continually playing catch up to make up for the time you lose when you keep putting things off. In such a situation it is common to always have work that you need to take home with you because you have a deadline to beat.

To avoid burn out, you need to have a daily ritual that helps you leave work at work. This means not taking work home with you because that is the time that you need to recharge and rejuvenate. If you get into a habit of always carrying work home with you, the possibility of burn out is very high because you are basically working round the clock. To prevent this a wind-down ritual can help you leave your work at work.

If you find yourself always preoccupied with thoughts of work even when you are at home, it means you are not winding down at the end of your workday. Detach from your workday by spending some alone time either relaxing or on a hobby that has nothing to do with work. When you get home take a relaxing bath, spend time with your children or just pick up a book you enjoy. Shifting your mind away from work helps you to minimize the pressure you are under and gives you time to do other things. Do not let work be the only thing in your life.

Even the most hardworking people fill their lives with other passions and this helps them to stay stress-free. Resist the urge to keep bringing work home. The more rested and rejuvenated you feel in the morning, the more efficient you will be during the day.

4) Keep your days structured

Nothing is more stressful than having lots of things to do and not knowing where to start. When you bring more structure into your day, it gives you better control over your time and resources. Having a schedule helps you to do as much as possible within the time that you have to work with. A schedule reduces the tendency to procrastinate and helps you to make decisions faster. That feeling of being overwhelmed that you get when you have so much to do and not enough time will dissipate when your day has a structure to it.

Learn to create schedules and time tables with a prioritized list of the tasks that you need to accomplish. Planning gives you better control over your day and makes time management much easier. Be vigilant about sticking to the schedule as this will give you the discipline you need to beat procrastination. A schedule will also allow you to be more productive. It will also help you manage the amount of work you are takin on so that you are not overworking yourself.

5) Identify your stress triggers

It is important to analyze yourself and find what tends to cause you the most stress. Is it an impending deadline, or overdue projects, or conflicts? Whatever it is that has you wanting to pull your hair out, it is time to either get rid of it or handle it. Stress builds up when you do not deal with the underlying cause of the pressure that you are feeling. If you are constantly feeling overwhelmed by your work, look for ways to either reduce the workload or delegate some of the tasks.

When you pay close attention to the things that wear you down, you will feel more in control of your life. This will reduce the amount of stress you have to deal with. Do not be afraid to say no when your plate is already full or to ask for more time if your schedule is overbooked. Running yourself rugged will only leave you feeling worn out and resentful especially if you never voice your concerns.

Do not let stress become a permanent fixture in your life by ignoring or refusing to address your stress triggers. You can only be productive if you are in the right mental state. Do not overwhelm yourself just to play along when you are clearly struggling to keep up. Sometimes something as simple as having an honest conversation with your superior or colleague can help you avoid needless stress.

Optimize your Environment for Productivity

Have you spent hours looking for a file, or trying to get an important contact that you misplaced? Procrastinators spend a lot of time either looking for things or distracted by things that are not important. Your work environment can either enable you or hinder you. Something as simple as organizing your workstation can make you more efficient. The simple truth is that chaos generates chaos. The less organized you are the less efficient you will be.

Your work environment should enhance your productivity. This means no clutter, no distractions, and having an organized way of arranging your work materials. If your workspace constantly looks like the scene of a crime, it could be the reason why you are not as productive as you should be. If you start off doing one thing then suddenly find yourself spending an hour or more just trying to locate something, your work environment is not optimized for productivity.

It may seem simplistic but working in an organized space makes your brain more efficient and reduces distractions. This does not just apply to your office workspace. The more organized your home is, the less stressed out you are likely to be. An organized space fosters calmness and a sense of being in control while a chaotic environment can make you feel overwhelmed. Managing your environment is therefore essential in boosting your productivity and helping you deal with procrastination.

Tips for optimizing your environment for productivity

- *Declutter*

Decluttering is one of the simplest ways to bring some order back into your environment. Get rid of things that you do not need or use. You can put them in your bottom drawers if you plan to use them in the future. If you have things that you are never going to use such as old files or memos, archive or shred them. The key is to only have things that you need or use. This also goes for your PC. If your PC is littered with files and folders that serve no purpose, all they do is clutter your workspace.

Arrange your workspace in such a way that the things you use constantly are within reach and those that you do not are put away. The effect of decluttering on your mind is almost immediate. Once your space is free of clutter you will start to feel more in control and confident.

- **_Minimize distractions_**

If you are prone to procrastination then you know that it takes only a little distraction for you to completely lose track of what you need to be doing. Keep your environment optimized for productivity by getting rid of distractions. This means if it is your phone that interrupts your work-flow, keep it on mute or switch it off. If music tends to make your mind wander, do not work with the radio on. You know what causes you to lose focus, so whatever your distraction is, remove it from your work environment.

Something as simple as staying off social media during work hours can have a significant effect on your productivity. When you are constantly getting distracted, it takes you time to get your mind refocused on what you were doing. This means that you end up losing plenty of time switching from one task to another. An optimized environment is one that enables you to focus on what you should be doing without constant interruption.

If you work from home, designate a workspace that is free of distractions and interruptions. Remember that procrastination is as much about not having the focus to do what you need to as it is about avoiding tasks. Even if you have the best intentions, if your workspace is filled with distractions, you are not likely to get much done.

- **_Have a to-do list_**

Winging it may work well if all you are doing is having some fun but when it comes to productivity, having a plan is crucial. Do not just get up and show up with no particular plan for your day. Get into the habit of creating to-do lists and schedules for the day.

When you create a to-do list, it allows you to prioritize the most important tasks that you need to do each day. This will help you overcome the tendency to put things off.

When you do not have a to-do list, it is very easy to get caught up with busy work that is not important or relevant to your goals. Have a plan for your day that reflects what you want to achieve in the short term and the long term.

Planning takes the guesswork out of your day and gives you better control over your time. Most of the time you procrastinate because you prioritize unimportant tasks over the things that really matter. A to-do list can help you schedule tasks in such a way that the most important things are handled first.

- *Make use of technology*

With all its faults, technology also has some great applications that can help you optimize your performance. Time management apps, schedulers, appointment setters, calendars, diaries and so many other apps on your phone and PC are dedicated to making your work easier. You do not need to be a whizz at time management to optimize your work environment. Making use of the available technology can help you increase your productivity and reduce the amount of stress you have to deal with.

If you tend to forget important appointments, simply put reminders on your phone. You can also use your phone to create and maintain a daily schedule to make the best use of your time. Explore beyond the social applications and find productivity apps that you can use to improve your performance.

Chapter 7: Mental Models

The man with only a hammer in his tool chest is bound to treat every problem as a nail. Simplified this adage means that you can only use the tools that you have at your disposal. The more tools you have the better equipped you are to deal with any situation that arises. This concept holds true for your thought process as well. Your ability to see opportunities and tackle challenges will always be defined by the range and flexibility of your thought process. The more limited your thoughts are, the more limited your options will be.

Procrastination is as much a thinking problem as it an emotional one. Your emotions whether positive or negative are always influenced by your thoughts. When you have positive thoughts natural you feel good. Similarly, negative thoughts will trigger negative emotions. These impact of thoughts on your mood is what makes it possible to have moods that have nothing to do you're your current circumstances.

If you close your eyes and think about something sad that happened to you in the past, the thought itself may be sufficient to bring tears to your eyes. On the flip side if you close your eyes and think about a happy memory, instantly your mood lifts. The connection between thoughts and emotions is always proportional and you cannot have negative thoughts and experience positive emotions.

In essence, the emotional resistance that you experience towards certain tasks, decisions, and responsibilities stems from the thoughts and perspectives you have. If you think a certain subject is difficult, you will be more likely to have emotional resistance to it because you have created a negative association in your mind. Your perspective is what influences how you feel about tasks, opportunities, and challenges. It can make you either confident and proactive or indecisive and prone to procrastination.

Your reluctance to start working on something is often driven by what you think. If you think it is easy you will be optimistic and eager to get started because you are not afraid to fail. On the other hand, if you think that it is beyond your abilities, your self-doubt will lead to the fear of failure and cause you to procrastinate. This means your perspective plays a significant role in your tendency to procrastinate and put things off.

Perspectives are like opinions and everyone has a different one. But what defines your perspective? What makes two people faced with the same situation see two totally different things? To understand perspective, you must first understand your thought process. The thought process behind your perception of how things work is referred to as a mental model. These mental models form the foundation on which you base your ideas, thoughts, and decisions.

The mental models that you use are created by your experiences, your beliefs, and by your understanding of the world. This means that all of us have different mental models that have been influenced by our unique experiences, beliefs, and attitudes in general. This explains why perspectives differ from person to person and why even when looking at the same exact thing, people will have different interpretations of it. Your thought process is unique because it is shaped by your unique experiences and your understanding of life.

Are you Limited by Your Thoughts?

A mental model is like a filter through which you see the world. It skews how you interpret things and informs your decisions and choices. This means if your mental models are limited, your thinking and perspective will be equally limited. The main difference between proactive people and people who procrastinate is that people who are proactive see opportunity where procrastinators only see challenges. This difference is occasioned by the kind of mental models that you use to perceive situations.

In the workplace, your ability to perform effectively will largely be determined by your understanding of your own role, how this role interconnects with those of your colleagues, and ultimately how your function contributes to the general objectives of your company. Having a clear understanding of your place in a system is essential for personal growth, understanding of the opportunities available to you, and for creating sound relationships. This means your productivity will also be influence by your perspectives and understanding of the people around you.

Your brain uses mental models as filters to simplify complex concepts and information. Since the brain is not capable of handling all the information and details, we see in the world around us, it creates models to simplify this knowledge into a thinking process that we can understand. In effect the more mental models you have in your brain, the broader the understanding that you will have of the world around you.

Your ability to make decisions benefits is only as good as the range of mental models you have at your disposal. If you can see a situation from multiple perspectives instead of just one, you will be able to make more informed decisions. However, if you only work from one perspective, your options will often be limited by the narrow perspective you are working with. This limited thinking is what causes you to look at a task and decide, *this is too hard, I will work on it some other time.*

When you have a broad base of mental models to direct your thought process you do not take things at face value. You can see beyond the challenge to the opportunity and you can see failure as a part of success. When your thinking is not limited to a narrow perspective you have the mental clarity that you need to get over the fear of failure and overcome the tendency to procrastinate.

Thoughts are catalysts for a self-fulfilling cycle. For you to achieve anything in the real life you must first conceive it in your mind. Most of the things you do well are the ones that you think you are good at and, not surprisingly, the ones that you fail at are the ones that you deem difficult. Your reality is a construct of your thoughts so you can never really reach beyond the limit of your thoughts. This means that if you do not pay attention to the mental models that direct your thought processes, you will create invisible barriers to progress and success.

Self-limiting beliefs are borne out of an inability to think beyond our experiences. If your perspectives are strictly based on your experiences and beliefs, then these perspectives are not objective. If you have a failed relationship in your past, can you then decide that all relationships are bad and not worth the trouble? Of course not. All situations are different and it would be irrational to use one relationship as a yardstick for all relationships.

Yet, when it comes to our abilities and beliefs, we do exactly that. You take something that happened in your past and use it to judge all future occurrences. You botched up a presentation a month ago so any chance to work on another presentation is met with trepidation and hesitation. You failed your midterms last year so every exam feels like it is an opportunity for failure and so on. The truth is we are constantly using our past experiences to make decisions about the future. The net result is that you procrastinate about the things that you fear and you embrace whatever seems easy.

This self-limitation is what happens when you use a fixed set of mental models as the basis for your thinking and decision-making processes. Mental models are essentially thinking tools. This means that the more you have at your disposal, the better your decisions will be. You are not restricted to the mental models you have acquired from experience. Since your thought processes are not static, you can increase your mental models and adopt new ones to give you broader perspectives.

A mental prison is every bit as restrictive as a physical one. If you want to see things differently, achieve new heights, and change your outcomes the way to do it is by changing the way you think. This means adopting different mental models and getting rid of self-limiting beliefs. Ultimately your adaptability and willingness to go beyond your beliefs is what will help you conquer habits such as procrastination that are driven by limited perspectives.

Tips for overcoming self-limiting thoughts

Question your beliefs

Stop defining yourself in terms of what happened or the mistakes you made. Labeling yourself limits your imagination and restricts you to your comfort zone. Do not take one incident and use it to define who you are. Calling yourself a loser, a failure, stupid, or any other label you use to talk yourself out of doing things is self-defeating.

Any new challenge or opportunity is a chance for you to prove yourself. if you let past experiences intimidate you, you will never have the courage to go after what you want. Strip the labels away and view each challenge as its own experience and not an extension of your past. just because your last job did not work out does not mean that every subsequent job will go the same way. Failure is an event not a way of life, so do not let it be who you are.

Adopt new mental models

Opening yourself up to new opportunities and experiences requires that you first adopt new ways of thinking and perceiving situations. The easiest way to get rid of self-limiting beliefs is to replace them with new ones. Acquiring new mental models will not only broaden your view of life but will make it easier to break old thinking habits.

Your ability to overcome procrastination will ultimately come down to your willingness to change your perspective and embrace new ways of thinking. This means expanding your range of mental models and replacing the ones that are only limiting you.

Re-Framing Your Mental Models

Your mental models are essentially the default settings that you use to operate. In most cases, you make choices within a split second because your mind is usually already made up about something. You never really stop to think, *I am going to dislike this,* or *I will like this.* Since you already have preconceived notions about most things based on your mental models you rarely ever stop to think about your instinctive reactions.

This means that it is very easy to keep making choices simply because that is the way you have taught yourself to think and believe. You will often tell yourself; *I am not good at that* or *this is too challenging* or *I don't feel like doing that*. Yet, these are conclusions you make even before you get started.

If you have already decided something is too difficult before you start, you will look for ways to avoid it or postpone it. This is how mental models significantly impact your productivity by causing you to procrastinate. Your default reactions cause you to become close-minded. This makes you feel like you are destined to fail or mess up in some way. Without even being aware of it, you create an invisible wall that stops you from going after what you want because your thoughts are holding you back.

You select facts from your experiences. You then assign meaning to these facts and use them to form the basis of your beliefs. These beliefs then become the yardstick that you use to judge situations. Essentially this means that your perspective is framed based on the facts that you choose to form the basis of your beliefs. When you look back at your past there are undoubtedly mistakes. Yet, in your past, there are also victories and things that you did right.

Unfortunately for procrastinators, the tendency is to only pick the facts that support your weaknesses. This means that you chose to remember the mistakes but you forget the victories. Ultimately this creates a thought process where the possibility of failure is always higher than the possibility of success. With this kind of negative mentality, it is no surprise that you become prone to procrastination.

The conclusions that you make are typically based on the facts that reinforce our beliefs. If you look at a situation, the only things that will stand out to you will be the ones that confirm what you already think. This is what makes self-limiting beliefs a self-perpetuating cycle. You will tend to ignore or overlook anything that challenges your beliefs because for all intents and purposes your mind is already made up.

This kind of bias when approaching situations is what clouds your objectivity and gives you a lopsided perspective. This means if you always feel like something is holding you back when you try to go after your goals, more often than not what is holding you back is your perspective. That is why to overcome procrastination you must be willing to reframe your mental models and embrace new perspectives.

Tips for reframing your mental models

Inversion thinking

Naturally, we are inclined to plan for what we want to happen. If you want to be a doctor you go to medical school, when you want to win a marathon you train your body for the event and so on. The principle of inversion is thinking about what you want to achieve in reverse by considering what you don't want to happen.

Inversion helps you to avoid the fear of uncertainty by giving you something else to focus on. If you have to give a speech in public then probably your mind is on whether you will be audible, articulate, and well-received. If you were to use inversion thinking in this scenario instead of thinking about what to do you would focus on what not to do. So essentially you would look for the things that would make your speech ineffective and take them out.

Inversion thinking simply gives you a different angle from which to approach a challenge so that it is not so daunting. Using this method of reframing can help you beat procrastination especially when you are not sure what to do. start by figuring out what not to do and this will inadvertently lead you to what you need to do.

Having a broad perspective is all about thinking outside your normal range. It opens you up to different opportunities by showing that there is always more than one way to tackle challenges. If one does not work you simply try something else until you start making headway.

Second-order thinking

Second-order thinking is a tool for reframing your thought process where you weigh the consequences of your actions before you act. This kind of reframing is especially useful if you tend to procrastinate as a result of the pleasure principle. Before you give in to the need for instant gratification, ask yourself, *then what?* This question triggers second-order thinking where you are not just thinking about what to do but also what the consequences of your actions are going to be.

For instance, if you are torn between finishing your assignment and going out with friends. Weigh the pros and cons of each choice. If you go out with your friends you will have a good time but you may not finish your assignment. If you fail to finish your assignment you will have free time today but tomorrow you will have two assignments to finish. When you view your situations with the possible outcomes it becomes much easier to make the right decision.

Second-order thinking prompts you to think beyond the immediate outcome of your actions to the consequences of these actions. This makes it one of the most effective ways to overcome the tendency to procrastinate.

The Bayesian Method

The Bayesian method is a statistical theory where probabilities express the level of belief in the occurrence of an event. When this principle is applied to thoughts, it involves considering all probable outcomes and scenarios. This means that if your standard approach to a challenge is, *what if I fail?* you need to consider the probability of success as well. This means turning your default reaction from *what if I fail?* to *what if I succeed?*

When you increase your list of probabilities you also increase the range of options available to you. Do not have the same list of probability for every situation you come across. When you limit the range of possible outcomes, you effectively feed your fear of failure and make it easier to procrastinate. In any possible situation, there are multiple possible outcomes that will depend on your actions. Focus on the probabilities that are closest to the outcomes that you want to achieve.

When you constantly update your field of probabilities you create more realistic scenarios and possible outcomes that are not tainted by your beliefs or bias. This objectivity can help you overcome self-doubt and the inaction that leads to procrastination.

Pareto's principle

Time management is one area where almost all procrastinators struggle. This means that finding an effective way to reframe your perspective when it comes to time management is crucial if you are to become more productive. Pareto's principle stipulates that 20% of the work you do typically generates 80% of your results.

This means that the majority of the work you do, 80%, only yields 20% of the results. In a nutshell, if you waste too much energy on all the wrong things you miss out on the important work that gives you 80% of the results.

This principle applies to time management by encouraging you to prioritize tasks based on their importance and relevance to your goals. It is very easy to stay busy with tasks that are not important while neglecting things that actually make a difference in whether or not you achieve your goals.

Your priority list should be based on the results you get from each task. The tasks that have the most impact on your goals should always be top of your list. The tasks with the least significance should be at the bottom of your to-do list. This principle is very important if you procrastinate because procrastinators tend to distract themselves with unimportant things to avoid tackling challenging tasks.

The 80:20 rule helps you determine exactly where your time and energy needs to go. Reframe your thinking to reflect your priorities and make sure that the decisions you make are geared towards accomplishing the most important tasks first.

Adaptation

You cannot successfully apply old ways of thinking to new situations and expect to succeed. New challenges call for new strategies and decision-making processes. In the wild, species adapt or die. This means that to survive, a species must evolve to keep up with the changes in its environment. Adaptation is not just a natural fact of life but it is also a requirement for productivity.

When you keep trying to do something the same way over and over again despite the fact that it is not working, you are essentially banging your head against an invisible wall. If your beliefs are no longer serving you or working for you the natural solution is to change them. Yet, time and time again people keep holding on to self-limiting beliefs that are leading them nowhere. This stubborn refusal to change leads to stagnation and prevents you from leaving your comfort zone.

It does not matter how hard you work if you are working hard at the wrong thing. The old adage, only fools do not change their minds, aptly captures the futility of refusing to adopt new ways of thinking. With experience and time, you learn, you grow and these experiences should inform your thoughts. If you are not learning anything new or picking up new perspectives constantly then you are doing yourself a disservice.

Do not be afraid to embrace new perspectives and ways of thinking. Your beliefs are only valuable if they are helping you get what you want. If the thoughts and values you have are no longer serving you, it is time to update them.

Use the why model

Why is a pretty mundane question but nothing is as effective in building self-awareness as a simple why? The power of why lies in the ability to make us question our actions, beliefs, and values. Self-analysis is not the most comfortable of endeavors but if you never question your thoughts and emotions, you are bound to keep making the same mistakes over and over again.

To beat procrastination, you need to get to the root of your hesitation, your fear, and your motivation or lack thereof. When you question your motives, you can begin to unravel self-limiting thoughts that are holding you back from your goals. Ask yourself why later, why not now? Why am I afraid of this decision? Why did it take me so long to act? Why am I always behind schedule?

Your self-destructive thoughts will only come to light when you question your beliefs. They will help you understand why you do things a certain way. Once you have these insights then you have a better grasp of the underlying issues. No one procrastinates just for the sake of it. However, if you do not dig deeper you may wind up thinking that you are just lazy.

When you understand the reason behind something, it becomes easier to question your choices and make better decisions. Do not just take your thoughts and emotions at face value. In most cases, the answer to your problem lies in the why.

The Decision-Making Process
The quality of your thinking will always be directly proportional to the range of mental models that you use to filter information and judge situations. If you are a one-trick pony whose thoughts are driven by fear or insecurity, your thoughts will not be able to go beyond the confines of your comfort zone. Just like you need an array of tools in your toolbox to handle any situation, you also cannot go through life with a limited mindset.

When you lack a broad set of mental models to facilitate your thinking, the net result is that you develop blind spots that make you biased in your decision making. If you have only one perspective, you are incapable of seeing things from a different angle so essentially you will just keep making the same mistakes over and over again.

For procrastinators, the issue in decision making is not that they do not know what the right thing to do is but rather that they cannot overcome their base instincts. When your emotions are the driving force behind your decisions then procrastination becomes inevitable. Emotions drive you to seek instant gratification which in most cases means putting off the things you need to do and indulging your impulses instead.

Procrastination is a habit that arises from the kind of decisions you make daily. You choose what to do, what not to do, and what to postpone. This decision is usually based on your thought process and the kind of perspectives that you use to judge situations. This means that for the decision to change, the perspective that you are working with must first change. To make better decisions and defeat habits such as procrastination you need mental models that empower you to make objective decisions.

Mental models for better decisions

Ditch the herd instinct

When it comes to peer pressure, unfortunately, most of us succumb to the need to conform. The herd instinct is driven by the natural human desire to belong and be part of something. However, this instinct can cause you to lose sight of your goals because you are too preoccupied with other people's thoughts and opinions.

To overcome procrastination, you need to have a clear dedication to your goals that is not tainted by other people's beliefs. This means cultivating independence of thought. The more dedicated you are to your goals, the less likely you are to falter in the face of challenges or opportunities. Think of how many times the thought of opinions or judgment from others made you too scared to go after something.

The truth is, your goals will never be completely in sync with those of the people around you. We all want different things from life and if you spend your time trying to keep up with the Jonases, it is your goals that are going to get lost in the process.

Make your goals the bigger picture that you are always focused on. When you have to make a choice between pleasing others or your goals, choose yourself. Remember that opinions are fleeting and you will never really win everyone's approval. The goalposts will always keep changing and they will always be something else that you need to do to fit in. So, screw opinions, and stay on the ball. Your life should be a reflection of what is meaningful to you and not what others think.

When you pick up other people's goals and discard your own, chances are they will not inspire enough passion or motivation in you. The net result will be procrastination because you cannot really be fully invested if the goals you are chasing are not your own.

The paradox of choice

With every extra choice that you have, the decision gets harder to make. If for instance, you have two job offers, it will be much easier to pick one than if you are trying to choose from five offers. Keep your options limited and your decision-making process will be much faster.

When you have too many options, the decision becomes too difficult and you end up procrastinating or not taking any action at all. Keep your choices limited only to the most important things and remove the rest from consideration. When you give yourself too many options you are only increasing the amount of time that you need to make a decision.

The number of choices you have also proportionately increases the probability of making the wrong decisions. To make your decision-making process fast and more efficient, keep things simple by limiting the number of choices you consider.

Control the controllables

If your decision-making process is always bogged down by worries of things you cannot control you will always be indecisive and prone to procrastination. Proactive people focus on what they can control. The truth is, there will always be things that you cannot control, but this does not mean they should impair your progress.

Stop getting cut up in the external circumstances and focus on your own actions. Life will always unfold as it will, and if your response to the unexpected is to let it stop you in your tracks you will make very little progress towards your goals. Your decisions should not be in reactions to what is happening around you but rather in service of what you are aiming for.

Circumstances have a way fo distracting you and making you lose sight of what you were working towards. Stay focused by shutting out the external noise and taking control of the things you have control over.

Your outcomes will always be determined by your individual choices and how you react to circumstances. Stop waiting for things to fall into place or for all your ducks to line up in a row before making a move. The more you focus on the things that you can control the greater the power that you will have over your outcomes and your life.

Chapter 8: Staying Focused

The possibility of future success is not always a big enough motivator to help you stay focused on your goal. When something seems out of reach or intangible it loses its hold on you. It becomes something that you think about but have no real attachment to. This is why you often go against your better judgment and put off things that you know will benefit you in the future.

Lack of focus is one of the most common reasons why people never realize their objectives. When you start off on a new goal or task you usually have a lot of passion and dedication to it. You spend a lot of time working on it and making sure you are ticking all the right boxes. However, as time goes by, your passion starts to wain and your efforts become lackluster. Gradually you stop caring about the goal altogether and you find yourself back right where you started,

The thing about focus is that it is only possible when you are still attached and invested in what you want to achieve. When this attachment starts to wane, your focus quickly follows suit. Think of all the resolutions you probably make every start of the new year. You start off all guns blazing and promising yourself that you will see your goals through no matter what. By mid-February, if you are still hanging on it is by a very thin thread if at all.

This tendency to lose focus and give up on our goals is what makes procrastination a habit rather than a one-time thing. Once you get into the habit of giving up, it becomes an easy choice whenever things get hard. Focus is what keeps you attached to your goals. Once the focus is gone, then the goal becomes nothing more than a pipe dream that you used to have.

Energy, as they often say, flows where attention goes. The moment you allow distractions to make you stray from your goals, then your mental and physical energy is misdirected from what is important to the distraction. No matter how hard you try you only have a limited amount of time and mental reserves. This means that when you are focused on distraction, the important things are not getting your time and attention.

Consider someone who gets so caught up in office politics that their job performance starts to suffer and they eventually lose their job. When this person first got employed, they probably had grand ideas about developing their career and becoming the best at what they do. Somewhere along the way something comes up and takes their attention away from their goal and they start using all their energy on distractions. Before they know it, they have completely lost sight of why they started working there in the first place.

This scenario repeats itself many times over in your life. You start to do something with a clear purpose in mind. However halfway through it, something else comes along, and your attention shifts. Without realizing it you start pursuing something that is not even that important to you and all your energy is wasted on things that do not really matter. The trouble with maintaining focus is that there are always plenty of distractions waiting in the wings to take your precious time and energy.

Keeping focus is not just essential in overcoming procrastination but also in terms of reaching any of your goals. If you cannot aim your energy in the right direction, somewhere along the way you will get distracted and find yourself right back where you started. Focus makes the difference between where you are now and where you need to go. Without it, there is no path from here to there.

Negative Energy

Nothing kills your focus faster than negative energy. When all you can see in your future is failure, then there is nothing to inspire you to keep moving forward. Imagine waking up every day thinking of just how bad your day is going to be. From the very first thought, you have to the last, the recurring theme is either how bad things are or how bad they are likely to get.

By the time you have had breakfast, you have thought about the horrible traffic you will have to sit through, the meeting with your boss that is bound to go badly because you missed your deadline and the overdue bills that are still sitting in the kitchen counter. These thoughts stay with you throughout the day, tainting every decision you make and influence how you behave.

If you start your day with this kind of energy what are the chances that you will have the drive to do the things that you need to? Of course, your motivation will be at an all-time low, because even before you step outside the door you have already visualized just how bad you are going to be. The trouble with negative thinking is that it tends to creep up on you without you being conscious of it. All you will really notice is that you are always in a lousy mood.

Negative energy leads to procrastination and interferes with your ability to stay focused on your goals. It makes you the perfect candidate for giving up because after all, all you can see is doom and gloom. People with negative energy always see the glass as half empty and never half full. That is why when confronted with a challenging task you will most likely put it off because you expect to fail.

If you tend to catastrophize everything then you will be in a constant state of inaction. Negativity is not just bad for your productivity but it also significantly increases the stress levels in your life. The more stressed you are, naturally the harder it becomes to stay focused.

Sometimes the negative energy you feel can be a result of your surroundings or the people around you. However, in most cases, negative energy tends to be a direct result of your own thoughts and beliefs. If the dominant thoughts in your mind are of failure, then the resulting emotions will be negative and you will be powerless to change your energy from negative to positive. Negative energy starts with your thoughts and goes on to encompass your emotions.

If you are a keen believer in Murphy's Law that anything that could go wrong, will go wrong, this kind of negativity may be costing you more than you think. Every time you are too afraid to seize an opportunity or take a risk due to negativity, you miss out on the opportunity to reach new heights and realize your dreams. Negativity is not just a mood but it affects how you do things and your ability to make sound decisions.

You may not always be aware that you are overly negative. Sometimes the distinction between pessimism and realism can be easy to miss. However, if you are not sure whether you are just in a bad mood or whether you generally have negative energy, here are the top signs that indicate you have negative energy.

- ***You are always complaining***

People with negative energy constantly complain about everything. There is always something wrong and nothing is ever quite right. This tendency to complain is caused by an inability to see the positive side of things. When you have trained your mind to focus on the negatives, you will always see the cons before you see the pros.

It is one thing to complain once in a while, but if you keep finding things to whine and complain about, this is a pretty good indicator that you have negative energy.

- **Is your vocabulary mostly negative?**

Your vocabulary says a lot about your thoughts so if you find that your speech has more negative words than positive, you probably have negative energy. If you often say things like *terrible weather*, *horrible traffic, stupid boss, nasty colleague* and things of that nature, chances are it's not them it's you, who has the problem. Negativity makes you prone to finding fault in others.

- **You like to play the victim**

Negative people often find comfort in playing the victim. They are quick to find fault and blame others for their outcomes. They rarely see the missteps in their own actions and often attribute their failures to others or circumstances. If you have negative energy then you often think that you are unlucky or that other people are out to get you.

In a nutshell, negativity is a way of looking at life that allows you to expect and accept failure and then blame it on others. With this mentality procrastination because very easy since you are always expecting a negative outcome. If you cannot turn your negative energy around, you will waste a lot of time looking for scapegoats while your goals get further and further away from you.

Negative energy will hold you back by diverting your focus from what you need to be doing. It forces you to focus on things you cannot control and this makes it impossible for you to remain in control of your life. If you adopt the belief that everything that is happening to you is a result of other people's actions or circumstances then you become helpless to change your outcome.

The 3-step process for clearing your negative energy

1. Take ownership of your life

Sometimes taking responsibility for your actions and your outcomes is one of the most empowering things you can do for yourself. Assess where you are in your life and understand that whatever position you are in good or bad, is as a result of the choices you have made. When you take ownership of your life it means that you give yourself the power to change it and create the kind of outcomes you want for yourself regardless of what the circumstances are.

Stop reacting to external forces or letting them influence how you feel about yourself or your abilities. External factors only affect if you allow them to become significant. Part of taking ownership of your life is realizing that no one else should be responsible for how you think and feel.

2. Change your perspective

If things look all gloomy and dark from where you are standing, maybe it is time to change where you are standing. Your bias can hinder you from seeing things objectively so sometimes it helps to shed your beliefs so that you can see things more clearly.

Always try to see things from a different perspective. If it helps ask a friend or colleague for their opinion. This way you will understand that there is always more than one perspective and that you can always change yours if it is not getting anywhere.

Do not take your perspective to be gospel truth. Remember a fixed mindset retards progress while people who are open-minded have a better chance of reaching their goals because their minds are open to new ideas.

3. Change your self-talk

Much of your negative energy comes from the kind of things you say to yourself. *You are such a loser, you will never get it right, why would they pick you, you have no skills,* it is amazing how self-critical we can be of ourselves and still expect to get things done. When you are constantly berating yourself, focusing on your weaknesses, and questioning your abilities, your self-confidence will plummet and you will always feel like you are not good enough. This will lead you to procrastinate and become too intimidated by opportunities.

Change the way you talk to yourself and this will change the way you feel about yourself. be kind to yourself by practicing self-empathy, if you would not say all those mean things to your friend why do you say them to yourself? people who manage to stay focused on their goals are those that cheer themselves on. They acknowledge their progress forgive themselves for their mistakes and focus on the positive.

Your thoughts become reality and there is no way your dominant thoughts can be negative and your reality positive. Thoughts influence your actions and behavior so tuning into the kind of self-talk you indulge in can help you stem the negativity and switch to a more positive frame of mind.

Ditching Bad Habits

Procrastination is a habit and like many other bad habits, it impedes your ability to reach your goals. Bad habits are like a shadow that follows you around sabotaging you every step of the way. Think of how procrastination turns your productivity upside down yet you still keep on doing it. Even when you know just how much procrastination is costing you, you always find yourself falling in the same pitfall and suffering the same consequences.

Habits are not just patterns of behavior. They are patterns that have become so deeply ingrained in how your brain works that you do them almost as a reflex. This means that habits are initiated by the subconscious mind which makes that much harder to control and stop. However bad habits can be ditched and replaced with good ones. If procrastination has been preventing you from staying focused on your goal, you can replace this bad habit by creating a new one in its place.

All the bad habits in your life are patterns of behavior that you developed as a coping mechanism to deal with something else. For instance, people with substance abuse problems, turn to these substances to deal with mental or emotional stress. When they are triggered by negative emotions, they are compelled to remedy their distress by turning to a substance that momentarily eases their pain.

Procrastination is also a habit that you develop as a mechanism to help you deal with negative emotions such as the fear of failure. Whenever you are faced with a task that you find challenging, you put it off because it makes you uncomfortable. This discomfort is what you try to avoid by constantly delaying action. Just like in the case of substance abuse, bad habits may give you a temporary reprieve from emotional distress but sooner or later the chickens always come home to roost.

When you procrastinate, the task or responsibility does not go away. In fact, you are only prolonging your agony by having it hanging over your head longer than it needs to. Whatever it is that you did not do today, will still need to be done tomorrow. The only difference will be that you will be under much more pressure tomorrow because you are running late.

This is the fallacy of bad habits; they present a temporary solution to a permanent problem that only gets bigger with time. No matter how well you tell yourself that you do under pressure, procrastination will always have a downside. Apart from the obvious cost in terms of time, the amount of pressure you have in your life will keep gradually increasing as the number of tasks that need to be completed keeps multiplying. Ultimately you will end up burnt out and unable to focus on your goals because you are mentally and physically exhausted.

Tips for ditching bad habits

- Replace the bad habit with a good one

The most effective way to ditch a bad habit is to replace it with a good one. This starts by you identifying the trigger that sets off the bad habit. if you procrastinate because of stress then the substitute for procrastination should be something that helps you deal with the stress. This means when you feel daunted or intimidated by a task or a decision, take a few minutes before you start to destress.

This can be anything from simple breathing exercises, to going for a walk or engaging in any other form of physical activity. The activity does not really matter. What is important is that you channel the negative emotion in a healthy way that allows you to still do what needs to be done. Look for habits that are productive that nonetheless help you deal with the trigger that drives you to the bad habit.

- Know your triggers

Your negative habits are set off by triggers. These triggers are the underlying emotions that you seek to assuage by indulging in a bad habit. some people for example drink when they are stressed. In this case, the trigger is stress. If this person is not stressed, they will not feel compelled to drink. In every bad habit, the trigger is the most important aspect to understand because it sets the behavior in motion.

Do you procrastinate when you are doubting your abilities? If that is true for you, it means that your trigger is self-doubt. Therefore, to ditch this habit, you need to deal with the self-doubt that is causing you to lack the confidence to move forwards. If your trigger for procrastination is poor time management, then to overcome procrastination you must first unravel why you have trouble managing your time.

The trigger sets of the chain reaction and is therefore the cause of your bad habits. If you can eliminate the trigger it will be much easier to ditch the bad habit. Bad habits are ultimately the effect and not the cause. To stop the effect, you must first deal with the cause.

- Visualize your success

the most effective way to stay connected to your goals is by visualizing themselves. Do not just have a vague idea of where you want to be in the future. Actively visualize it in your mind and make the image as clear as possible. If your goal is a promotion, actually visualize yourself sitting in the corner office. Make your goal not just a far-off idea but something tangible that you can look forward to.

Bad habits are able to keep their hold on you when you are not driven enough to stay on track. When you visualize your goals, you give it the power to motivate and discipline you to stay focused. Many people use vision boards for this very reason. When you can wake up in the morning and see the thing that you want to achieve, it is no longer just an idea but something tangible.

Ditch your bad habits by visualizing the success you will achieve without them. Even just visualizing how relieved and accomplished you will feel after finishing a task can help you to overcome procrastination. When you feel the temptation to postpone or delay things just imagine what it will feel like when it is done. When you stay connected to your goals by visualizing them, you effectively cultivate the kind of focus that you need to stay committed.

- Get an accountability partner

Having someone to share your progress with is a great way to stay focused and overcome bad habits like procrastination. That is why having a work-out buddy can sometimes help you stick on a diet regimen that you are unable to stick to on your own.

A support system does not just provide external motivation. It also helps you to feel responsible and accountable. When you know someone is watching and cheering you on, you are more likely to do the right thing because it is not just about you anymore. Let a close friend or colleague know what your goals are and share your challenges with them.

Sometimes just talking things over can help to put things back in perspective and enable you to maintain focus on your goals. If you can do it on your own that's great but there is also nothing wrong in getting a support system to help you achieve what you want.

Getting Comfortable with Uncertainty

Neuroscience tells us that our brains, much like water flowing downstream in a river, will always take the path of least resistance. Think of a pianist who spends hours and hours practicing her craft and honing her skills. Or an athlete, who will train for hours on end before the day of the big event. The more they practice, the better they get and the easier the actual performance becomes.

The more you repeat an action, the stronger the neural pathway linked with that particular skill becomes. This is why every skill you have learned over time gets easier with each subsequent repetition. This premise goes beyond just physical skills, the path of least resistance influences our actions, habits, and behavior. For risk-averse people, it is not just a decision that they make but rather a way of thinking that becomes entrenched over time.

If you examine your life you will realize that your behavior and actions tend to follow familiar patterns. This is simply due to the fact that the actions you repeat over and over, become entrenched neural pathways that create the path of least resistance that your brain takes in any given situation. So, when you say that's just the way am wired or I am set in my ways, it is not just the surface characteristics but your very way of thinking and making decisions.

If you have spent all your life as more of a thinker than a doer, you will not suddenly wake up one day raring to go. Procrastination and indecision become entrenched with time and become harder and harder to break. If your mind is geared to always veer in the direction of the least risk or to keep the status quo, undoubtedly most of the decisions you will make will reinforce this belief.

This means that to achieve anything you must first conquer yourself. Over time you have developed a set of beliefs and expectations that influence the way you make decisions and how you look at life in general. Are those beliefs serving you well or are they holding you back? Have you internalized fear of the unknown to a point where you are stuck with brilliant ideas that never got beyond the corners of your mind?

Self-disruption means getting to the crux of the matter excuses and uncovering overcoming the fears that may be holding you back from changing course. Going after what you want often takes guts and confidence and these two things can be only be cultivated by disrupting the ideas and beliefs that hold you back.

It is easy to think of changing the world. Changing yourself, not so much. Stepping outside your comfort zone and entering the world of uncertainty is the first step towards change, growth, transformation, and the pursuit of possibility. Every time you choose not to act, you are allowing your fear of uncertainty to distract you from your goals. People who are proactive are not necessarily the most brilliant or intelligent. What actually sets them apart is the courage to take chances and go after what they want.

Procrastinators always have a good idea of where they want to go. What stops them from making progress is their fear that the outcome may be different from what they envisioned. Uncertainty makes you uncomfortable because it is human nature to seek comfort and security. When anything threatens your comfort, your first instinct is to avoid it because you do not want to disrupt your life.

While comfort may seem like the safer option, comfort also means that you are not making progress. There is no progress that is made by standing still. To move from where you are now to where you want to be you must be willing to make a move. This is why embracing uncertainty can help you get over the tendency to procrastinate and avoid anything that challenges you.

The truth is, with great risk comes great reward. Most of the things you dream about exist on the other side of your fear. This means that if you keep letting fear stop you, you will never know what you could have achieved or how far you would have gone. Fear is one of the strongest motivators known to man and if you let it control you, you will always choose the safest path. Unfortunately, the safest path is not always the path to your goals.

People who succeed do so by making bold moves that push them to go beyond their comfort zones and face their fears. They understand that there is a possibility that they will fail but they choose to focus on the possibility that they will succeed.

The thing about uncertainty is that it is a feeling, not a fact. Unfortunately, just like many other emotions, uncertainty does not have to be based on facts to become a stumbling block in your path. Your fear of failure may stem from past experiences, a misconception of your own abilities, or even just something someone once said to you ten years ago.

Your fear of uncertainty may be justified or it may be inane or even absurd. However, in all these cases, it has the power to stop you from going after opportunities that have the potential to be life-changing. You could be David with a proverbial slingshot going against an impressive Goliath with all the odds seemingly stacked against you, but unless you take the first step, you will never really know how it would have played out.

When you train your mind to focus on all the reasons why it could go wrong, your ability to see opportunity becomes diminished by the fear of failure. This can lead you to not just procrastinate but also impair your ability to identify opportunities for growth and go after them. Ultimately the bigger your fear of uncertainty is, the more likely you are to procrastinate.

Tips for getting past your fear of uncertainty

Prepare and plan ahead

A boxer does not just walk into the ring with a hail Mary. He trains for his bout to get himself ready for the task ahead. In much the same way preparing and planning for the tasks you have to handle will boost your confidence and reduce the fear of failure. There is something about being prepared that makes you feel like you are up to the task.

Stop waiting for things to happen to you and start preparing for them instead. If you have a project coming up. Get yourself ready by brushing up on your knowledge consulting and generally making sure that you are ready to take on the task. Most of the time we get intimidated when we know we have not prepared adequately for what we need to do.

When you prepare and plan ahead, it will not completely eliminate the possibility of failure but you will be better equipped to handle the outcome. Taking control of the situation by preparing and planning will help you to stay focused.

Reflect on past successes

Fear is as much a mindset issue as it is an emotion. The more you focus on your mistakes the more your fear grows. In contrast, when you focus on your successes you build up your confidence and this helps you to overcome self-doubt. Make a habit of reflecting on your past successes whenever you have a challenging task ahead. This will shore up your confidence and help you move past the fear of uncertainty.

Ask for feedback

If you have worked on a project or task before, ask for feedback from others in order to understand what you did wrong and what you may have done wrong. When you have a clear understanding of where your strengths and weaknesses lie, you will know exactly how to approach the task ahead.

Sometimes when you are unsure of yourself, your fear of uncertainty increases because you do not know what to expect. Feedback can help you understand your blind spots because sometimes we do not always see our mistakes objectively.

Advice from Your Future Self

Hindsight they often say is 20/20. Of course, that's not saying much after all if we all had the luxury of working backward from the objective, there would be little room for error. In fact, Stephen Covey, in his book The Seven Habits of Highly Effective People, underscores the fact that always starting with the end in mind is one of the most efficient ways to reach your goals.

No matter what stage you are in life, you have picked up a few lessons along the way that have shaped your perspective and view of the world. But forget for a moment what you do know and project yourself a few years into the future. What advice would you give yourself? What do you think you have to do right now to get to that future that you have envisioned?

At the end of the day, no one knows better than you the ways in which you sabotage your own progress. Overcoming self-sabotage is important because you may not be able to control external circumstances, but you can certainly control your internal environment. Do you need to be less hung up on perfection? Are you too addicted to your comfort zone? Have you let opportunities pass you by because you were too afraid?

Whatever your issue is, self-awareness is essential for success in any field. You cannot hope to defeat anything else if you lack the ability to self-regulate. Take for example the perfectionist who has been stuck with a business idea for years but has not dared to put it out there because they are still trying to perfect it. Perfection is a fallacy that sets you up for failure fast. It will result in many missed opportunities as you waste time chasing an illusion.

When you have an idea that you want to put out into the market, your first concern should be achieving a minimum viable product. That means getting a functional prototype that you can get out into the market then tweak based on feedback. If instead, you focus on getting the perfect product, you will waste a lot of time on something that you may still have to adjust based on feedback. Chasing perfection does not just rob you of opportunities it also steals your time.

Time is the most valuable commodity you have. You can make more money, you can have more ideas, but you can never create more time. Time is a limited resource that if you do not use, you lose. Start now, start where you are, and start with what you have it is as simple as that. By being proactive and taking the first step, you save yourself a lot of time. Often, people get caught up in the details instead of acting. Preparing, planning, and forecasting are all well and good but it is taking action that will bring your idea to life.

There is no science to getting started, you simply have to do it. It may be scary at first but the fear can be your motivator or your hindrance depending on how you look at it. Cultivating a growth mindset will help you embrace uncertainty and all the challenges and victories that come with it. The most important thing when it comes to beating procrastination is to simply get up and show up.

This means that even when you are uncertain, doubtful, or downright terrified, you have to find a way to get past your fear. Yes, you may fail because failure is part of the journey to success. Think of failure as part of the process of achieving your goals and becoming better than who you were.

If you let your fear of failure stop you, then chances are your goals will always be nothing more than an idea. Grit and resilience will get you through what your skills and talent cannot. This is because the most important thing about failure is not that it happens but rather how you deal with it. When you can go through failure, take your lessons in stride and get back in the ring, you will have developed the kind of resilience that sets apart great entrepreneurs from the rest.

A major part of the fear of failure is the natural instinct to save face. Stop worrying about what people will say or think. We spend so much time fretting about what other people will say or think that we forget that people in most cases are too caught up in their own lives to give yours much more than a passing glance. Not everyone has to share your vision. If you are afraid of resistance or criticism, you will always falter in the pursuit of your goals.

Trying to impress others or show them up, is not only a waste of time but likely to lead you to make bad decisions. When you are trying to keep up with the Joneses, you are likely to either go too fast or go too slow. Learn to pace yourself. You want to take steps that are big enough to challenge you but not so big that you are overwhelmed.

Ultimately, nothing worthwhile comes easy. There will be plenty of reasons to quit, plenty of reasons to procrastinate but if you can keep your eye on the ball, the battle is already halfway won

Chapter 9: Habits for Success

How did I get here? Is more or less the universal creed for people who suddenly find that the shit has hit the fan and they have no idea when or how it happened. Now, if you have found yourself up shit creek with no paddle in sight then you probably know this feeling well. We are often bamboozled by our own lives and at times you will catch yourself thinking, *how did things get this bad?*

In this puzzle what we often miss is the fact that we take certain paths, make certain decisions, and operate on certain beliefs that map out the course that our lives take. The truth is every outcome in your life is a direct result of your habits. There is no getting around this fact. Where you are at this moment in your life is down to the habits you have created. How happy you are, how fulfilled or unfulfilled you are, and even how successful you are all tied to your habits.

It is human nature to always look to the outside for solutions, *I would be happier if my boss was nicer*, or *I would meet the girl of my dreams if I was luckier* or *I would have gotten that job if she was not so unreasonable,* or *this marriage would have worked if he was more considerate*. The list is endless. Every single day you find reasons why other people are responsible for the outcomes in your life.

We often cite circumstances beyond our control or bad luck or other people's actions and make them the reason why this or the other went the way it did. This self-delusion helps us sleep better at night. It absolves us of the responsibility for our mistakes and gives us a scapegoat to pin our failures on. Unfortunately, this kind of self-deception prevents you from taking control of your own life because you are busy waiting for luck or things to fall into place or for other people to be nicer to you.

It has been said often that you make your own luck. This means that the circumstances that you find yourself in will be determined by your habits. In a nutshell, your fate has always been in your own hands. The reason people have such a hard time understanding that their outcomes are a direct result of their habits is that most of the time people are not really aware of their habits.

Think of all the things that you do without really consciously thinking about it. Like what time you get up each day, getting coffee every day at ten in the morning, or going to the bar for a few drinks after work, or even eating when you are stressed out. These are not things that you actually stop to think about. You have gotten so used to doing them in a particular way that they are basically second nature; they just happen. These set patterns of behavior become your habits and your habits create your outcomes. It really is that simple.

Habits are the default settings that you have created for yourself. These things that you do repeatedly each day on auto-pilot determine who you are, your belief system, and your approach to life in general. This means that to change any aspect of your life, you must first change your habits. So, what habits do procrastinators get into that keep them from being productive? Well, procrastination in itself is a habit. When you become accustomed to putting off difficult decisions or tasks and avoiding tackling what you do not like, it eventually becomes a way of life.

Stop Self-Sabotage

What happens when your conscious and subconscious mind are at odds? When your rational brain is telling you to study for the test and your subconscious brain is telling you to play a videogame? When you want to eat healthily but an inner voice is pushing you towards a Big Mac? There is always an inner battle between doing what we know is right and doing what feels good. This battle is between our conscious or rational brain and the subconscious brain.

Your better judgment is the conscious mind that is telling you to study for your test while your subconscious mind is pushing you towards seeking pleasure and instant gratification. Your subconscious mind is all about reinforcing your beliefs, values, and emotions. If you are facing a difficult task, your subconscious will push you towards an easier or more pleasurable task. This avoidance of discomfort is what drives people to seek instant gratification.

When you need to get to the gym but there is an inner voice telling you to skip it and watch a movie instead, or when you have work to do but you end up choosing to hang out with your friends instead, these are routine choices that we make without realizing that our subconscious mind is sabotaging our conscious mind. We know what we should be doing, we know what is more important but somehow it just feels better to do something else.

To understand why this happens, you need to figure out what your subconscious is. The subconscious mind is made up of the thoughts, emotions, and beliefs that are always running in the background of your mind without you necessarily being aware of them. They are like the undercurrent that is pulling or pushing you to go in one direction instead of the other. Your subconscious steers your decisions much like the current in a river determines which way the water flows.

Your subconscious is a reservoir of sorts that keeps your memories, beliefs, values, and all the little things that make you tick. So, every time that you try to do something that contradicts what is in your subconscious, you face internal resistance because you are going against who you think you are.

Let's say you believe that you are poor in Math. Every time you want to study this particular subject you will face emotional resistance because you believe it is hard. So, you will find yourself putting off studying Math or avoiding that subject altogether.

Similarly, if you believe that your boss does not like you, every time you need to talk to him or approach him you will dread the encounter. This means that you will avoid talking to him unless it is absolutely necessary. Ultimately you start to get into a habit of prioritizing things that feel good or comfortable and ignoring more important things that challenge your beliefs.

Self-sabotage occurs every day on so many different levels. If you are unaware of the kind of thoughts and beliefs that you are holding in your sub-conscious you will always find yourself doing things against your better judgment. Overcoming self-sabotage starts with questioning your self-limiting beliefs. These are the beliefs that tell you, *you will never be able to accomplish this*, or *you cannot have that*, or *this is all you are ever going to be*.

These beliefs are the major reason why you procrastinate and avoid important decisions that have the power to change your life. For instance, if you believe that you cannot get a better job because you are under qualified, what are the chances that you will look for better opportunities? Almost none, because you have created a box in your mind of what you can and cannot do. this means that you will always be stuck in the same position since you do not want to risk challenging your beliefs.

This is how self-sabotage works, it starts with a self-limiting belief that then locks you into a little box that defines what you are capable of. This box then becomes your comfort zone and anything that threatens this comfort becomes a challenge that you need to put off or avoid in order to feel safe.

The longer you stay within this comfort zone the harder and harder it gets to change or challenge yourself. So, you become trapped in habits that are getting you nowhere simply because you boxed yourself in. That is what self-sabotage is in a nutshell; blocking the path to your goals and opportunities by giving in to self-limiting beliefs.

To stop self-sabotage, you must first become aware of your self-limiting beliefs. What are the things you say to yourself constantly? Are you always focused on what you did wrong, why you can't do this or that, or who does not like you? Your thoughts become reality so allowing a train of negative thoughts in your mind will chip away at your confidence and self-esteem until everything starts to feel like an impossible task.

Stop the negative self-dialogue and instead focus on positive thoughts and emotions. Even simple positive affirmations like, *I am talented, confident, and brave* can go a long way in boosting your self-esteem and confidence. Be your own best friend and cheer yourself on. Find your inner positive voice and strive to keep it. Negative thoughts will creep up from time to time but if you consciously make an effort to counter them with positive ones, you will gradually have more positive than negative ones.

Stop beating yourself up over mistakes you made years ago. Why is it so easy to have a fight with your friend in the morning and forgive him by lunchtime yet you are still blaming yourself for something you did three years ago? Practice self-empathy by forgiving yourself and allowing yourself to move on. Don't label yourself a failure because you failed at something in the past, take your lesson from the mistake, and move on. The more you learn to accept and love yourself the fewer self-limiting beliefs you will have.

A simple way to get past self-limiting beliefs is to do something you would never do. Volunteer to take lead on a project in the office, go for that blind date you have been dreading, or start jogging in the morning. The more you stretch out of your comfort zone, the more confident you will be and the less likely you will be to put things off because they scare you. Remember fear is at the root of procrastination but once you prove to yourself that nothing is too difficult, this fear will start to dissipate.

Declutter Your Mind
Carrying around tons of mental baggage is not just exhausting but will often leave you feeling overwhelmed. To do the things that you need to do, you first need to create mental space by decluttering your mind and freeing it from mental baggage. Most of the time when you end up putting off doing important things, it is because you feel that you already have too much going on.

Imagine if you had to walk around all day with a backpack full of baggage on your back. When you wake up in the morning this backpack is strapped on your back and when you go to bed the backpack is still strapped to your back. Not only would it be exhausting to live that way, but the baggage that you are carrying around would keep getting in the way of everything else that you need to do.

Mental clutter is essential baggage that you carry around in your mind. You have it with you when you wake up and you still have it with you when you get to bed. It gets in the way of you getting things done because it is constantly weighing you down. The longer you carry this clutter around the less room you have for the important things. You become chronically stressed and always feel overwhelmed by the sheer amount of mental baggage that you are carrying around.

Decluttering your mind relieves mental stress and fatigue. This gives you mental clarity and the ability to make decisions and do what you need to do. Fortunately, getting rid of mental clutter is possible if you follow these simple strategies.

Simple tips for decluttering your mind.

1. Prioritize

Prioritizing simply means defining what is most important. Write down a list of the things that have the most significance in your life in terms of achieving your goals, your productivity, and your overall well-being. You can make a list of priorities for the day, for the week, and so on. This means every day when you get up you have a clear purpose and set of goals to work on.

Prioritizing helps you in two major ways; it gives you focus and it helps you to stop sweating the small stuff. When you have clearly defined priorities procrastination stop being an issue because you are always clear on what you need to do first.

2. Avoid multi-tasking

When you try to do too much at once, you reduce your efficiency and this ultimately affects your productivity. Tackle one task at a time following the priority list you created. Not only will you be more efficient, but you are also going to be free of mental clutter.

The more you overwhelm yourself, the more likely you are to procrastinate so avoid this by doing one thing at a time. Most people think multi-tasking saves you time but it actually takes you much longer since you have to divide your focus and attention.

3. Be decisive

Mental clutter is usually a result of things that we have delayed to do or make decisions on. Start by creating timelines for yourself to make decisions. Look at all those things you have kept on hold like unanswered emails, proposals you have not responded to, or buying decisions. Sit and consider each at a time.

Give yourself a fixed amount of time to weigh the pros and cons of each pending decision and come up with the way forward. The more decisions you make, the fewer the unresolved issues you will have, and the less the mental clutter you will have.

4. Talk to someone

Sharing your thoughts can help you to relieve mental pressure and address issues that are weighing on your mind. Talk to a friend or someone your trust and share your thoughts often. The more you open up, the lighter you will feel. You may not always get a solution from talking, but sharing your thoughts can be liberating.

5. Breathe

Deep breathing is a simple but effective technique to clear your mind. Take deep breaths before you start working on something or when you feel overwhelmed. This will help to clear your mind and reduce mental clutter.

Instant Gratification Isn't So Gratifying

It is no secret feeling good, well, feels good but if you make a habit of prioritizing pleasure then don't be surprised if your outcomes are below average. When your decisions are made based on the easy way out or on the least uncomfortable option possible, you will often miss out on all the great opportunities that come cloaked in a bit of difficulty.

Nothing worthwhile comes easy and unfortunately to get what you want from life you must be willing to work for it. This means that before you put off doing something because it is hard, or boring or simply because you would rather do something else, consider the consequences.

Sure, skipping the gym means you will have more time for drinks with your friend but how will you feel looking at your fat ass in the mirror in a month? Skipping class to go on a date, is definitely more pleasurable but how will that D look on your transcript? Most of the time when we give in to the need for instant gratification, it is because we have not stopped to consider the consequences.

Patterns of behavior become habits and these habits determine how far you will get in life. It may seem like an innocuous decision in the moment, but every decision you make tends to have consequences down the road. So always ask yourself if what you chose will be worth the pay-off you get in the end.

When you are tempted to do what feels good instead of what is important, remind yourself which one will matter a week or a month from then. You will probably not remember the show you watched instead of studying, but the D will still be on your transcript a month and even years later.

Avoiding or putting off difficult tasks or decisions only makes them harder to do in the future. When you choose to indulge yourself, the pleasure is usually fleeting at best, and then sooner or later you still have to get back to reality. If you struggle with instant gratification you can turn things around by changing the script. When you succumb to the need for instant gratification, you are essentially rewarding yourself before the work is done. Flip the script by rewarding yourself after you have accomplished what you need to do.

When you make the reward or pleasure a consequence of the action and not a substitute for it, you will essentially be motivating yourself to act. It can be as simple as buying yourself a new outfit after you finish the work project or going out for a drink with your friends after the exams are done. In this way, you still get the reward but it comes after the work not before.

Develop Self-Discipline
The key to overcoming bad habits and changing your outcomes will ultimately come down to self-discipline. Are you able to regulate your impulses and your emotions? If you cannot control your self then there is very little chance that you will have any real control over what happens in your life.

Habits are formed when we reinforce certain behaviors repeatedly. For instance, if you tend to binge eat when you are stressed out, this behavior follows a predictable loop. First, there is the trigger which in this case is stress. Then this trigger is followed by a certain behavior or reaction, in this case eating. Finally, after the behavior, there is a reward, which is the comfort you get from food.

Once you have created this loop from trigger to reward, then your brain follows that same path every time you are stressed. That is why habits are so hard to break. It is because they become entrenched in loops that only require a particular trigger to set them off. The only way to break these habits is to change the reaction to the trigger. For instance, in our example above, if when you feel stressed you go for a walk instead of eating, then the loop you had established previously starts to break and your mind does not automatically go to food when you are stressed.

Self-discipline starts with self-awareness. What do you do habitually that stops you from getting things done? Do you waste time planning or preparing just to delay the start of difficult tasks? Do you distract yourself with other things so you do not have to deal with the real issue? When you identify what your trigger is and the subsequent reaction, then you can start to break the loops you have created in your mind.

Eliminate the distractions and temptations that keep you from doing what you need to be doing. Switch off the phone when you need to be working, remove the junk food from your refrigerator, or just get rid of anything that tempts you or makes it more difficult to focus on your goals.

Sometimes eliminating distractions may mean knowing which friends or co-workers distract you from your purpose and make it impossible for you to pursue your goals. Be brutally honest with yourself when it comes to identifying all the distractions you allow to keep you from working towards your goals.

Have well-defined goals that you have identified and determined as important for your progress. This will give you something to work towards and make it easy to recognize and say no to distractions. It is hard to get anywhere when you really do not know what you want out of life.

At the core of self-discipline is the ability to manage your emotions. Do not do things because they feel good, or because they are easy. If you take this path you will always be reaching for the low hanging fruit. Get comfortable with challenging yourself and being uncomfortable. Remember the only way to empower yourself to change your life is to first have control over yourself. Know which of your impulses sabotage your progress and which ones push you forward.

Chapter 10: A New Beginning; Your Tools at a Glance

Change is difficult because it makes us confront all the things, we do not like about ourselves or our lives. When you look at the relationship that has been stealing your joy for years or the job that has stifled all your creativity, it forces you to acknowledge painful truths about the decisions that you have made over time.

For most people change is daunting because you assume that you need to do a whole 180-degree turn or make a complete overhaul of your life. However lasting change is possible when you take small and deliberate steps each day to change your situations and be the person you know you can be. This means that instead of looking at change as this really big mountain that you need to climb, think of it more as a series of small steps that will get you to different milestones and eventually your ultimate goal.

If you struggle with procrastination and getting things done, all it takes is empowering yourself with the right tools to overcome this self-defeating habit. Understand that you can change the way you think, change your beliefs and as a result change your outcomes. Every day presents a new opportunity to choose a different path and start a new journey.

If you do not like where you are right now, you do not have to stay in that situation. Just like your habits got you to where you are now, you can create new habits to get you to where you want to go. These simple but effective tools will be your most important weapons against procrastination. Use them well and you will realize that there is really nothing stopping you from achieving your goals.

The Power of Self Awareness

How well do you really know yourself? When you make a decision do you understand why you have made it or do you simply do things because they feel right? Any new beginning starts with a willingness to self-examine and understand ourselves.

Are you happy with the way things are going? How have you contributed to the situation you are in? What beliefs do you have that hold you back from getting what you want? What do you really want out of life? Are you doing anything to get there or are you simply hoping things will fall into place? What three things are you putting off that could possibly change your life?

These questions may be unsettling, but they will help you to take stock of your life. If you are simply going around operating on autopilot, you will have a hard time achieving any meaningful change in your life. You must be willing to dig deeper and find your fears, your flaws, your strengths, and everything in between.

The more you go behind the curtain, the easier it will be to unravel negative thoughts, self-sabotage, and bad habits. Do not seek to change what you do not understand, first understand, and then seek to change those habits attitudes and beliefs that do not serve you.

Simple strategies to cultivate self-awareness

1. Practice mindfulness.

Life can get hectic sometimes and it is easy to be thinking about one thing while doing another. However, if you do this often, you start to lose touch with your emotions. When you are not in touch with your emotions you will not understand what causes you to act or behave in certain ways so you will be at a loss on how to change bad habits.

Strive to be more present in your own life and exist in the present. Simple techniques like deep breathing exercises or meditation can help you shut out the outside noise and focus on the present. Take deep breaths and focus only on the breathing until you feel centered and grounded in the present. This will heighten your self-awareness and help you to be more aware of your emotions and thoughts.

2. Keep a journal

Journaling is one of the simplest ways to keep in touch with your inner self. Keep a journal and write down your feelings. This will not only help you process your emotions better, but it will also give you a deeper understanding of why you think, feel, and act the way you do.

3. Ask for feedback

Do not be afraid to talk to people who you trust and ask for feedback. Sometimes seeing ourselves objectively can be hard so a friend may help you to see things that you are blind to. We all have our blind spots and getting feedback from people can help you see the things that you avoid.

4. Write down your goals

It is important to have a clear idea of what is important to you and what you are working toward. Your habits can only align with your goals if you know what those goals are in the first place. Do not just think them, write them down. Be specific on the timelines as well to make the goals more three dimensional.

5. Look at yourself objectively

Stop labeling yourself based on past mistakes or experiences. You are not the guy who botched the presentation, or the fat girl or the nerd or any other name you call yourself. Do not label yourself because in so doing you put limits on what you can and cannot do. Be objective and strive to leave the past in the past.

Maintaining Focus and Motivation
Without passion, your goals may very well be just writings on a piece of paper. To stay motivated and focused you need to be passionate about your goals. This starts by pursuing goals that are significant and mean something to you.

If you are simply going through the motions, do not be surprised if you keep putting off decisions or taking action. If something is really not that meaningful or important to you then it is no surprise if you do not feel motivated to work for it. Passion inspires us to work hard because what is on the other side is something that we really want and are willing to make sacrifices for.

So, are your goals important to you? Are the things you are working for meaningful enough to be worth all the work you need to put in to get them? Look at it this way, if you are working for something you do not really care about you will put in minimal effort. However, if your goal is something you always think about and yearn for then you will do everything to get to it.

Sometimes when you procrastinate it may be simply because you do not care enough about the payoff. If this is the case, then you will always have trouble staying focused and motivated. Start by setting goals that actually mean something to you and have real significance in your life. Once you have identified what those are, get rid of all the other things that you simply do to pass time or please other people.

Once you have these goals in place, make yourself accountable. This means letting a partner or a friend know what you are working towards. This will make you feel accountable not just to yourself but to someone else. The more accountable you feel the more motivated you will be to finish what you started. Remember motivation is both intrinsic and external. You can get motivation from the people in your life and in this way stay focused on what you are trying to achieve.

Simple Strategies for Motivation

I. Make sure whatever goals or objectives are your own. Do not work to meet other people's expectations of you or the goals they have created for you. Set your own goals that are meaningful to you.
II. Take care of your body and emotional health. The better you feel about yourself the easier it is to stay motivated. Eat right, get enough sleep, and make physical exercise part of your routine.
III. Visualize the reward. Nothing is as powerful as seeing yourself with the very thing that you have always wanted. This is why vision boards work. They motivate you to work even harder because you have already visualized the outcome of your hard work.
IV. Start small and keep it simple. One of the reasons people quit is when they feel overwhelmed. Break your goals down into smaller milestones that will help you chart your progress. Every time you achieve a milestone you will become even more motivated to stay on track.

V. Be consistent. Consistency is what will keep you going on the days when you are just not up to doing anything. When you establish a consistent schedule or action plan then you will find yourself doing it every day no matter what your mood is. Focus on creating consistent actions and habits that you can follow daily to achieve your goals. This will take emotions out of the equation and help you stay focused.

Time Management Strategies
One of the biggest casualties of procrastination is time. When you are perpetually stuck in limbo because you cannot bring yourself to make a decision one way or the other, time just keeps passing you by.

Why are there people who by the age of twenty-five have achieved great things while others even at forty are still trying to figure their lives out? It has more to do with time management than brilliance or cognitive aptitude. People who can manage their time well will naturally get more things done.

For people who procrastinate the amount of time spent avoiding things or putting off decisions becomes costly in terms of time. So, one of the best ways to overcome the trap of inaction and procrastination is to develop better time management skills.

Simple strategies for time management
I. Make a to-do list every day. List all the things you need to get done daily. This gives you a clear plan of what you need to work on that day.
II. Prioritize your to-do list. The most important things should be first on your list. Then work your way down the list.

III. If you have any unpleasant tasks or difficult tasks, do them first. When you finish the difficult tasks, you will be more motivated to take on everything else on your list.
IV. Give yourself timelines. Your goals for the day should have timelines. Make each task and assign it a time limit. This will help you avoid spending too much time on a single task.
V. Take regular breaks to help you stay focused and avoid mental fatigue. It takes you more time to finish something when you are mentally exhausted so taking regular breaks will help you stay sharp.

Psychological Tricks to Stop Procrastinating

1. The five-second rule

If you are prone to procrastination then you know that the longer you take thinking about something, the more hesitant you get. So how do you get past this? Simple just count down from five and start. This method doesn't give you time to find excuses or reasons not to do it. So, every time you have a difficult task ahead, do not stop to think about it or to let it marinate in your mind, simply count down from five then start.

2. Break the avoidance loop

If you have been staring at a blank computer screen for a while or whatever task it is you need to do, break the avoidance loop by starting afresh. Go for a walk, take a shower, change location, or do something else for five minutes. This will help you to get past the mental block you are facing and overcome the resistance that is hindering you from starting.

3. Create artificial pressure

Some people work best under pressure so unless they feel like they are under the gun they will procrastinate until the cows come home. So, if you are in this group, create pressure for yourself to get moving. Place a bet with a friend that you will finish by a certain time, or promise yourself a reward if you complete the task by a certain time. Motivating yourself this way helps you to act and prevents procrastination.

4. Start small

Fear is one of the main reasons people procrastinate so one of the best ways to overcome indecision is to start small. Break down the task into small manageable steps then work your way up until it is done. Most of the time you will find that the first step is usually the hardest, after that your confidence and motivation increase as you go along.

Create a plan of action that starts with small but deliberate steps. This makes the decision or task more manageable and easier to process. You do not want to intimidate yourself into inaction so start small and start with what you can handle.

5. Get your shit together

Isn't it weird how life seems to follow Murphy's law? When things are going great, they are really great but on some days everything that could go wrong goes wrong? The more control you feel over other areas of your life the more confident you will feel about tackling difficult tasks and getting things done.

Chances are that if your home life is falling apart, sooner or later your work will start to go to the dogs. This means that it is important to have your shit together if you want to successfully overcome procrastination. Start by fixing the small things and work your way to the bigger tasks. Something as simple as organizing your desk can make you feel more confident and more in control over your situation. Do not let one area of your life affect every other aspect of your life. If something is not working as it should, find a way to fix it or get rid of it. You will never be fully focused and in charge of your outcomes if you are dealing with psychological distress from failing relationships, poor health, or financial woes. Get your shit together and you will find that things that seemed so hard are not as challenging as you thought.

Conclusion

Hindsight as they say is 20-20 and often when we look back on how we have gotten to the point we are in, we can clearly spot the missteps that we made along the way. However, since you have no time machine to take you back to the past to make different choices, all you can really do is work for a better tomorrow.

It does not matter how much procrastination has set you back over the years, we are all works in progress that have an opportunity to change every single day. So instead of dwelling on what you could have done and all the opportunities you missed, focus instead on what you can achieve by being more proactive and decisive every day.

The most powerful enemy you have is the one within so the only person that can stop you from being who you want to be is the one in the mirror. Acknowledging that there are areas where we fail and sabotage our own progress is often difficult but it sure beats going down like a defective parachute.

No matter how far you think you have fallen, there is always a way to get back up and rewrite your story. If most of your life has been about putting off important decisions and avoiding things that you do not like, you now have all the tools and knowledge to turn this around. This can be the day that you take a small but sure step to change your outcomes and live the life you really want.

By reading this book you have already taken a small but deliberate step in the right direction. All that is left for you to do is to start applying the principles you have learned in this book. Remember that your consistency will be your biggest ally in changing from being a procrastinator to someone proactive and decisive.

Every day make small changes and set small milestones for yourself that slowly help you to unravel the negative emotions and habits that are holding you hostage. In every section of this book, there are useful tips and strategies that you can use on a day to day basis. It does not matter what stage you are in life, your age, or even what you do, the principles for overcoming procrastination are universal and will help you now and in the future.

We hope the information in this book will bring you closer to your dreams and help you live a better life.

SPECIAL BONUS

3 video courses 100% free!

- Bulletproof Mind
- Mindpower Mastery
- Success Habits

Get instant access here:

(just copy and paste this link into your browser)

>> https://bonus-academy.com/free-courses

Printed in Great Britain
by Amazon